BELLAIRE AND BILLY

BY

BILL LOVETT

Drawings by Author

ISBN: 978-1-4269-5471-9 (sc)
ISBN: 978-1-4269-5472-6 (e)

Trafford rev. 02/08/2011

 www.trafford.com

North America & international
toll-free: 1 888 232 4444 (USA & Canada)
phone: 250 383 6864 ♦ fax: 812 355 4082

BELLAIRE AND BILLY –
FOREWORD

This book is being written solely from memory by the writer, of incidents and conversations exactly as they happened back in the 1940's and 50's. In some cases names are original and not changed because the dialogue is truthful and not fictitious or slanted. There is absolutely no malicious intent to embarrass or slander any individual portrayed in this historical recollection of life and events in Bellaire at that point in time.

A famous person once said; "A man is not a man until he has planted a tree, built a house, fathered a son and written a book". So this completes the circle for me, and I have finally reached the age of maturity. It certainly took me long enough but I was in no hurry because I didn't want to admit to old age too quickly. You see, completing the circle has a sense of finality to it that is not very appealing to one's senses!

I want to forewarn you that there are some passages here that some of you may consider "raunchy" or "colorful" according to your individual point-of-view. They weren't written that way for shock value but to give you a more truthful and clear understanding of the feelings that I experienced as a naive young boy without prior background or knowledge of them.

I thoroughly enjoyed the writing experience and discovered as I went along that one memory led to another, and another, and another and I had no idea what a total pleasant feeling of accomplishment and fulfillment it would bring to me. I know that some of you will consider this book to be a "rag" and throw it in the trash, but hopefully some of you will enjoy the trip back to the past for what it was intended to be. — "Bon-appetit".

Chapter One: The Move

March 14th, 1945 was a cold, blustery day in St. Clair Shores, Michigan. Not freezing weather, but just cold enough for the occasional wet flurry to maintain the inch or two of snow still on the ground where shallow snow banks lined the roads. It wasn't deep, only a foot or so, but enough to tell you that winter was not yet ready to give up the ghost. It was hardly a good day, to say the least, for a long trip and family move to northern Michigan. My parents, Lloyd and Amanda Lovett, had both worked in the war effort during World War Two. They had saved a fairly sizable amount of money and had planned for some time to make a change in all of our lives and begin a new venture in northern Michigan in the log cabin business. They believed this new direction would be a great life experience for all of us!

I was ambivalent about this change in my life. At 12, puberty confused me. I loved animals, especially horses for some reason and every chance I could get I shoveled manure at the local riding stable so that I could ride my favorite steed for free a couple of hours each week. Upon returning home, I would be confronted by my mother who shrieked, "Billy!, Don't you dare wear those shoes in this house"! You see, shoveling horse manure is a learned skill and a lot easier if you used the inside of your left shoe to block the stuff as you pushed the shovel against it with your right hand. With a lot of experience I had become pretty adept at it, much to my mother's disdain. Somehow, she didn't appreciate this newly acquired skill as an integral part of my formal education. But what can I say, I liked horses!

And then there were girls! (not to be compared with horses, of course.) Although I had a sister, Yvonne, who was two years older than me, we were constantly fighting and I simply could not understand how this female could be such a witch and most of the others I met were absolutely fantastic! I fell instantly in love with nearly all of them that were around my age (I think.) I wanted to do something with them! I wasn't quite sure what, but I know I wanted to hug them, kiss them, feel them up and then what? That part of my education was a little fuzzy though progressing rapidly. But I digress. Getting back to my story;

The 250- mile trip to northern Michigan was fairly "ho-hum" with just a couple of exceptions. The further north we went, the nicer the weather! Strangely, it turned into a beautiful sun-shiny day and became progressively warmer. Now how could that be? Normal intelligence dictates that the further north you travel, the colder it gets, right? What is wrong here? In retrospect, that was the first clue that there was something mysteriously magical about our family's move to a charming little town named **"Bellaire."**

The other incident was, well, a little different. It was if God was saying, "hey there, not so fast, let's balance things out here a little bit." Our old 41 Hudson was running beautifully, taking our little family of five unceremoniously north at a pretty good clip. A very smooth ride, considering we were also pulling a 2- wheeled trailer loaded to the gills with furniture and other family necessities. **Then, suddenly**, as we were cruising down a long hill just south of the little town of Roscommon, mother said, "Lloyd, look at that wheel passing us over there in the field!" "Where do you suppose that came from"? As we all gaped at the unbelievable sight, reality struck with a lurch, and a long grinding noise! That strange wheel had just come off of our trailer!

Now my father was a large, strong man, but it was almost all he could do to wrestle the Hudson to a safe stop alongside the road. Back in those days, there was no such thing as power steering except for your own power and strength to do the steering. Thank heaven mother wasn't driving at the time or that may have been the end of all of us! Dad passed away 25 years ago but I still recall in wonder how innovative he was in his ability to get the job done, no matter what the task.

He hitched a ride into Roscommon and within an hour he was back with new wheel bolts to replace the broken ones that had worn through from the weight of the trailer load, and we were on our way again.

I still marvel at some of the things my father accomplished. I guess when you have lived through the "Great Depression," you learn how to manage with what you have or what you can scrounge up. Dad was not afraid of hard work and liked to do things with his hands. Like the year he decided to build us a new house during the 2nd world war. Building materials were very scarce, but dad worked at Hudson Motor Car Co. and every day he brought home packing materials from the auto parts they had been shipped in. He brought home wooden crates and felt paper that normally would be discarded and he used them for the house. He single- handedly built the new house around the old one, then dismantled the old one, piece by piece and threw it out of the upstairs window! And he did that while we were still living in the house and in the middle of the winter! Sounds ludicrous, but it worked just fine for us.

When we arrived in the little town of Bellaire late that evening, we unloaded our things into the house. It was dark and we were all tired so it wasn't until the next day that we had the chance to explore our new home. My parents had purchased an entire estate that had belonged to a deceased lumber baron. It consisted of a huge house in town and a 260-acre farm just west of the village limits. The acreage encompassed a mile and a half of lake- front on lake Bellaire and one and a half miles of river frontage on the Intermediate River. All of this being a part of the renown " **Antrim County Chain of Lakes**". Dad had this dream to have his own business and had taken on a partner he had befriended in the Detroit area. His friend Milton had also moved his family to Bellaire and together they formed a new company, named the "**Bellaire Log Cabin Mfg. Co.**" The company became successful and distributed kit log cabins across the country for over 40 years. Some of the early ones can still be found in and around the Bellaire area.

Unfortunately, in a short time, my father developed an allergy to the Cedar logs they used in manufacturing the cottages and he was forced to sell out to his partner after just a few years. Dad regretted not being able to pass the business on to his sons, but so goes life. Fate gets tipped one way or the other and life goes on.

Chapter Two: The New Home

The morning after the trip we arose from a good night's sleep and began to examine the house. Mother was elated! She had been raised on a large farm in rural Wisconsin with eleven brothers and sisters and she had learned to cook on an ancient wood stove. " Ooo-la-la," this old house had two of them, one in the parlor to heat the house and one in the kitchen for the cooking and baking. Dad wanted to tear them out immediately and install modern systems but mother would have none of that! She agreed to change the heating system but insisted on keeping the elaborate chrome -lined wood stove in the kitchen. Of course this meant she needed an endless supply of wood to feed the stove. Well, guess who had to supply that? All eyes turned to me, of course. Until then, although I had my share of house and yard chores, I had never touched an axe or saw. That was about to change. I was getting tall, about six feet at age 12 and although very slim I was all bone and muscle and over the next few months, would become very strong – <u>from chopping wood!</u> Now, believe it or not, although this big house was located in the middle of town, it also sported a barn in the back yard. The house dated back, of course, to the days before automobiles so the owner had to have a structure to house his horse and buggy. How else would one get about town? Problem – we needed wood to burn in the stoves. Solution – The old barn had to go and "Billy Boy" had to convert it to firewood!

Dad always had a back straining, muscle building answer for difficult problems. So my younger brother and I had the task of tearing the barn down, piece-by- piece, hammering the old nails out and cutting it to pieces. If we had only known how much that barn timber would sell for a few years later, I could have used that argument to save us endless hours of hard labor. But that isn't the end of the story.

In the back of the house was a separate but attached, unheated shed that was used as a rear entrance, wood storage and much to my glee, where the previous owner kept his fishing gear! Lots of old poles, reels, and baits! I had never been fishing before, but was desperately eager to do so, and our house was only one block from the Intermediate River. I will re-visit this interesting subject later, after the house tale is finished.

The house in town was three stories tall but the top story was unfinished and was destined to be the "boys bedroom" because, you see, even though there were four other bedrooms, initially we had to share living space with Milt's family including his three daughters. Now you might think this is an ideal set-up for a "farmer's daughter" kind of story. Unfortunately, for me, it didn't turn out that way. One of the girls, "Mary Lou", was my age, and a real "looker". She was sweet on me and I had a thing for her too. Did I ever! The problem was, our parents were very aware of it, watched us like hawks and we were never allowed to have five minutes alone together. It didn't take long for Milt to realize he couldn't manage the situation any longer so he moved his family out to the old farmhouse way before the re-modeling was finished. Mary Lou and I only had fleeting moments together during which we told each other dirty jokes but that was about the extent of it.

The first few days after our arrival in Bellaire, were spent exploring the house, the town and especially the farm with it's rolling terrain and water front. We enjoyed day after day of warm beautiful weather. The snow melted and flowers bloomed almost immediately. It seemed very romantic to me and gave me a euphoric, poetic feeling that I will never forget!

Bellaire is nestled in a secluded valley surrounded by Maple forested hills in the middle of the "Antrim

County Chain of Lakes". A small power dam on the river there divided the upper and lower chain of lakes. With a population of only 1150, Bellaire was a tiny town but also housed the county seat that was located in a red brick building, clock-and bell-tower courthouse that was built in 1905. Approaching the town from any direction, the first thing you saw was the tall clock- tower silhouetted against the surrounding hills. It was truly a magical, story-telling place to live.

Sometime during the first summer, as I have said, Milt and his family moved out to the farm and we were left to ourselves with the big house in town. Dad decided to put an oil furnace in the basement! I ask you, what basement??? There wasn't one under that house! That little fact didn't matter to dad. He would simply dig one! Now a job like that is hard enough before the house is built. That is the normal time to dig a basement, right? Well, my father was a remarkable but very stubborn man. He was bound and determined to teach his boys the hardest, most frustrating ways of accomplishing the dumbest things you would ever want to learn to do! Actually, when they were finished, some of these dumb jobs eventually were quite functional, like the basement. Now how did he (we) do it?

This house was situated on a large corner lot on the north of town. It had a spacious side yard centered by a gorgeous, huge, Douglas Fir tree with it's lower branches laying right on the ground. The tree was at least 60 years old at the time and it is still standing today so that would make it at least 120 now. It is in itself a Bellaire Landmark. Dad had to trim the lower branches of that tree so that he could accommodate the task he was about to undertake.

To begin, he cut a 6 ft long hole in the house foundation facing the side yard. Then using a shovel he dug out as much dirt inside of the foundation as far in as he could reach. When that was done, dad rented a horse named "Jack" rigged up with a big scoop from a local farmer. He backed the horse up to the hole in the foundation, crawled under the house, dragging the scoop in with him and situated himself on his knees in the cramped space behind the scoop. Try and picture this situation now as dad grabbed the handles of the 3 ft wide scoop and hollered out "GIDDY-YAP, JACK!"

"Well, the wind blew and the shit flew, and over the hill came Jack!" Actually, it was a little worse than that. Jack took off, causing the front of the scoop to dig in a little too deep, flipping the handle end upward and catching dad under his chin in the process. Luckily for him, the long handles slammed up against the floor of the house just in time before decapitating him or our family's time in Bellaire would have been cut a lot shorter! (no pun intended.)

If anyone in the neighborhood didn't know what dad was doing at that moment, they were soon to find out. The air turned blue for a couple of blocks in all directions as everyone learned some very nasty language. Some of which I am pretty sure, were not in their latest version of Webster's dictionary. I know dad had a lesson for me there, but I'm not quite sure just what it was.

Eventually, dad got the hang of it and proceeded to scoop out the entire basement and deposit it in our side yard. Somehow he was able to do that without the house caving in on top of him in the basement. I learned later there is a name for this type of structure. It is called a "Northern Michigan Basement." (how appropriate) After the dirt is scooped out, forms are built and concrete is poured in, forming inward sloping walls in the basement. This procedure is absolutely necessary because the northern Michigan soil is very sandy and dry, making it quite unstable without the sloping walls.

Scooping the soil out took several days and we ended up with a huge pile of dirt about ten feet tall in our side yard. Now what in the hell was he going to do with that? It didn't take long to find out as I braced myself for yet another "lesson"!!!

"Billy", he said, "we now have to move this sand out to the farm"!!! Really!! I knew he wouldn't just let me stand there and watch him work by himself forever. Problem – big pile of sand. Solution – big flat bed stake truck and two "idiot sticks" (shovels). One for dad, and one for "Billy Boy". Do you have any idea how many evenings under the light of the moon it took us to shovel all that sand into that stupid truck, cart it out to the farm and then shovel it out of the truck again?? It took for—e—v—e-r! It wasn't all that bad, though, there were some benefits. Over the next few months, I grew 2 inches taller, gained 4 or 5 inches on my biceps and legs, and several inches of muscle between my ears.

Finally, the great lesson came to me like a bolt out of the blue. "Get an education, stupid"! Don't ever do this sort of thing again! From then on, I vowed to always use my brains instead of my brawn.

Now, we had a huge hole under the house that had to be converted to a basement. So, with the help of a local contractor and a lot more shoveling, dad formed the walls with wood. Then they brought in a cement truck to pour the concrete through the hole in the foundation that had been used to remove the sand. After that was finished and the concrete had cured, there remained the task of installing the huge oil furnace into the new basement.

Originally, there had been a small fruit cellar under the house, accessed by a narrow stairway from the glassed in summer-porch. Unfortunately, the stairway was too narrow to accommodate the huge furnace. This little problem didn't bother dad. He just dismantled the doorway, jamb and all and made it fit. My recollection of the event was that it still took several men and my father to wrestle that humungous furnace down the stairway. As I recall, there were many skinned knuckles, much foul language and a lot of sweat to accomplish the feat.

It just so happened there was a benefit to me in this new stairway access to the basement. We now had an enlarged fruit cellar and mother loved to can fruits and vegetables that I loved to eat. So I was constantly up and down the stairs retrieving canned goods for us all. I was soon to find out of yet another benefit from the stairwell!

One Sunday afternoon Mother had invited friends over for one of her famous chicken dinners. As usual it was so sumptuous it just melted in your mouth. We were all sitting at the long table on the sun porch when mother asked me to retrieve a quart of canned peaches from the basement. As I started back up the stairs from the basement, I had a clear view of the underside of the dining table and was absolutely startled at what entered my gaze! My feet and eyes froze at the same time as I stood there dumfounded! The man's wife was sitting there facing the stairs. It was quite warm on the porch and she was sitting with her legs apart and the nice lady had no panties on! She was in her young forties and was still a good-looking woman. Actually, from my view she was absolutely fabulous and when her eyes eventually met mine, she realized she had unintentionally just greatly enhanced my sexual education. (on second thought, maybe it was intentional). She could tell I was grateful and gave me a coy little smile as I tried to hide my growing manhood. It seemed like it took me forever to regain my composure. Those things just don't go away that easily when you are a horny young teenager! I made some excuse to leave the table and it was some time before I could rejoin the others there. Somehow, thank-heaven, nobody else noticed my embarrassment and the sweet secret remained forever between the lady and I. (until now, of course).

Chapter Three: The First Summer and Fishing

My first summer in Bellaire was an enchanting time in my life. I had always dreamed about living in a place where I could enjoy the outdoor life of fishing and hunting and here I was, living in that paradise. Our house was only a block from the river and although I was yet to learn how to swim, I spent that first summer fishing from the old railroad bridge and the powerhouse dam that separated the upper and lower chain of lakes. The river averaged about 100 feet across but there was a pond just above the dam with a spillway to hold the excess water that wasn't diverted directly through the electrical generating plant. The spillway would be raised or lowered according to the upper chain rainfall so as not to overload the generators. Strangely enough, the electrical power generated was not used for Bellaire, but was transmitted by power lines 30 miles away to the town of Charlevoix! What a waste of energy that had to be for the distance of transmission. Years later the power plant was torn down and this inexpensive source of energy, was lost forever.

The pond above the dam contained about 40 acres of water, was only 3 to 8 feet deep and was full of old cedar tree stumps where the land had been forested about 100 or so years ago prior to building the dam. According to the Bellaire archives, there was an old" wooden-ware" factory located at the site around the turn of the century. More history on this can be gleaned from the Bellaire historical society if the reader so desires. Anyway, the tree stumps in the pond provided perfect cover for a variety of fish and the pond was full of them. It wasn't until later that summer that I acquired a boat so I had to do my fishing either from the railroad bridge that covered the expanse of the pond or from the spillway. I took to fishing like the proverbial duck takes to water and spent the majority of my time digging for worms and feeding them to the fish. (That's what I did, feed the fish!!) It took me a while to learn how to keep them on the damn hook so that the fish had to also take the hook and not just the worm. Eventually I caught on and made my mother very happy as I kept her in a constant supply of fresh fish. Mother and I had an arrangement. I would catch and clean them and she would fry them. At first, she cleaned them but after one wriggled when she began to clean it, she panicked and from then on I had to cut off the heads and eventually do all of the cleaning part.

Dad loved fish also, but for some stupid reason, he would not eat the ones I caught. His had to come from the store. I don't know if he thought I was trying to poison him, or what. So he missed all of the fresh fish and mother, my siblings and I had a banquet all to our-selves.

Later on in the summer, my uncle Merle came to visit from Indiana. Uncle Merle owned a large cattle farm near South Bend and like me, loved to hunt and fish. He had given me my first 22 rifle so obviously he was my favorite uncle. Northern Michigan was uncle's favorite vacation place and every year he would spend 2 or 3 weeks hunting and fishing in the area. One day during his visit he and I were watching the boat traffic from Warner Bridge on the Southwest side of town. We noticed an old man with a hand made rowboat complete with hand made oars tying up his boat under the bridge. Merle hollered at the man, "how much will you take for that boat?" The old man, a little startled, hesitated for a moment and then replied, "eight dollars!" "Sold!" uncle Merle said, and bought the boat on the spot and gave it to me! He didn't know at the time, but that generous gesture would have a very dramatic impact on my life. Over the next 2 years, I would row that boat up and down the river, across Lake Bellaire and into Grass River on countless fishing trips with my siblings and friends. This great exercise of rowing would build the muscles in my arms, legs and stomach until they were honed like tendons of steel. I was already tall and now became as strong as a bull. It was probably the most defining activity that resulted in my proficiency as an outstanding baseball pitcher in high school, college and beyond into the pros.

During that first summer in Bellaire, although I loved the fishing, I longed to have a friend that I could share my outdoor enthusiasm with. I didn't have long to wait. One day while fishing at the spillway, another boy about my age joined me casting from the shore. He introduced himself as David Allen and told me he lived on the South end of town with his schoolteacher mother. His dad had left the family years before and never returned. So he had no father figure or companionship to help guide him. Dave had an older sister that was already married and lived around the corner from them but that was all the family he had. Dave and I liked the same things in life and therefore became instant best friends.

One evening, we decided we would fish for Bass after dark on the pond. Around nine o'clock we gathered our gear, climbed into my boat and rowed to a spot we felt would be good for casting. I had quite an array of old Bass plugs that had been left in the house by the previous owner and

I proceeded to try them all out. Dave and I sat in opposite ends of the boat facing away from each other and began casting our lines. About my third cast, David yelled "ouch!" and I felt my line tighten before it was supposed to. It seems my back-cast was not yet perfected and I caught him beside the head just above his right ear. He would definitely be the biggest catch I had that night and for the rest of the summer too. Dave didn't see the humor in the situation but he wasn't in much pain because the barbed hook had only lodged under the skin. I tried my best to remove it, but it wouldn't budge. There was only one thing we could do! I had to cut the line and walk him all the way through town to the doctor's office.

Now David was a proud fellow. <u>He didn't mind the walk but he didn't want anyone to see him with that stupid Bass plug sticking out of his head!</u> The walk only took about fifteen minutes, but " **plug-head Allen"**, as he would henceforth be known as, insisted we take the long way through the dark alleys in order to further camouflage his new sporty headgear.

Old Doc Gervers maintained his office in his home on the South end of town. He was a good doctor but wheel chair bound due to a gunshot wound that paralyzed him from the waist down years earlier. Because of his disability, his practice was limited only to procedures he could perform from a sitting position. The good doc had been accidentally paralyzed in a gun battle during the infamous <u>Mancelona bank robbery</u>. He ended up being involved in a posse attempting to stop the robbers in their flight from the bank. As it turned out, the so-called robbers weren't the thieves at all but the Mancelona police chasing the robbers! The two forces mistook each other for the culprits and engaged themselves in a gun battle for some time before the mistake was discovered. Poor Doc Gervers became a casualty because of that stupid mistake. Remarkably, this little romantic town of Bellaire has a multitude of interesting stories like this. I certainly don't know them all but I'll entertain you with a few of them.

Doc Gervers removed the Bass plug from Dave's head and advised us that due to our lack of expertise in the sport, we should try and do our bait casting during daylight hours. We concurred and Dave smiled with the knowledge that he didn't have to hide in the back alleys of town anymore, even though he wouldn't outlive the story because I told <u>everyone</u> I knew about how "**Plug-head**" got his nickname!

And he was known thereafter as "Plughead Allen"

Chapter 4: Characters

As small as this town was with a population of 1150 people, it had more than it's share of unforgettable characters. The first one I met was Charlie Parks. Charlie was the town hermit! There was a beat-up old shack on the South shore of the Bellaire pond that Charlie called home. I don't remember if it had doors or not, but if it did, Charlie never closed them. Wild animals of all kinds wandered in and out of his house at their leisure and paid him no mind except for an occasional handful of food, which Charlie shared willingly. He only owned one suit of clothes, all black, except for a white shirt. His jacket, trousers, shoes and tall, stove-pipe hat were all black and with the exception of his waist length white beard, he looked a great deal like Abe Lincoln. Years before, he had somehow broken his left leg and didn't go to a doctor to get it properly set. As a result, the leg bent out awkwardly at about a 30-degree angle from the knee, which necessitated him to walk with a hand made cane. To my knowledge, he never spoke to anyone unless he had to, and then, only briefly. I encountered him countless times while fishing on the pond, both of us paddling our small fishing boats, looking for the best spot of the day for pan fish. I would bid him "good morning" and his only reply was a polite, but simple nod of his head and he would move on, rowing his boat ever so slowly. I pondered his simple existence and was intrigued by his character and life experiences that had molded him to this present being. I am sure his life story would have made very interesting reading.

Charlie was dirt poor, so I am sure the pan fish he caught, must have made up 90% of his diet as long as the pond wasn't frozen. I can only remember one time during the years that I lived in Bellaire, that I saw him walking in town with his cane, carrying a bag of groceries. He obviously had no income but somehow managed to get some food staples, as he needed them. Relatives routinely checked on him and one day they found him dead in his cabin. Cause of death was unknown and, to my knowledge, never determined.

Then there was old Charlie Sexton. There were several Sextons in town and Charlie was the older brother. My first memory of him was one Saturday evening in the summertime. As I was walking through town towards the "free show" on the river bank, I observed Charlie and his friend, "Dummy John" sitting on a bench in front of the Bellaire Bar watching the girls go by and spitting tobacco juice all over the sidewalk. **And I do mean all over**! We didn't have a movie theatre in town so a travelling "entrepreneur" with a projector and reels of old movies came to town every Saturday night and showed his films on a large wooden sign frame mounted on the vacant lot by the river. There were some makeshift benches and a few people brought their own canvas lawn chairs for more personal comfort. The projectionist was savvy enough to also bring a popcorn machine and cases of soda in order to profit from his labors. Most of the movies were pretty entertaining with the likes of Charlie Chaplin, Laurel & Hardy and The Three Stooges. Nearly a hundred people came to town every Saturday night to socialize with each other and watch the films. Rich kids from the summer camps on Torch Lake were there and mixed with the town kids for a few back-alley smooching and beer drinking trysts. At times this led to an occasional low-key "fist-fight" and kept life interesting!

Old Hermit Parks

Getting back to Charlie Sexton. He and Dummy John always parked themselves in front of the bar after getting slobbery drunk and being ejected from the interior as a result of their unruly behavior. A complimentary bench with accompanying spittoon was placed there for tobacco users.

The sidewalk was forever spattered about 6 ft in all directions around the spittoon. Charlie and Dummy, after getting slobbery drunk and being ejected from the interior as a result of their unruly behavior would place themselves on that bench. They would sit there, watch the girls go by and chew and spit until the cows came home. They would spit in the general direction of the spittoon, but the drunker they got the worse their aim became. Dummy John, obviously, was deaf and dumb and could not speak intelligible words. He would gesture with both hands, mumble and spit and somehow, enable Charlie to understand what he was trying to say. But after they were drunk, the mumbling, gesturing and spitting got worse and not much of the tobacco juice ever got near the dog-gone spittoon. As a result, the sidewalk there became pretty stained and slippery after a few hours on a Saturday night and when Charlie and Dummy finally decided to stagger home, they usually took a few prat-falls on their asses before they could stumble to their feet and make any worthwhile progress in a given direction. It was a hilarious scene to watch and more fun than the movies!

"Dummy John" was a tall, skinny fellow with no teeth. He lived in a small shack outside of town on Stover Pond Road and you could usually find him, (assuming you really wanted to), walking between his house and the bar. Try as I might, I could never understand a word he was trying to say. However, a lot of people in town, especially those who drank with him, could. Everybody liked John. When he was drunk, which was most of the time, he put on quite a show and he knew it. He would mutter, grunt, wave his arms and spit profusely, gumming his speech in an attempt to get you to understand and <u>always</u> extracted smiles and laughter from everyone around. When they saw him walking, most people would stop and give him a ride, especially in bad weather. John lived to be pretty old and as the story goes, they found him one winter day, frozen stiff along the road.

Charlie and "Dummy"

Pete Sexton

"Pete" Sexton was another one. After his ball playing days, he spent a little time in prison. I think it had something to do with his brief, failed marriage. " Non- payment of support, or something like that. I don't really know. But Pete was perfectly harmless. He had no driver's license and no need for one because he didn't have a car anyway. That didn't stop him though. He was always going somewhere and implored upon various townspeople to take him there. If they balked a little or tried to beg off for some reason, he became very insistent as though they "owed" him. At this point most people gave in rather than have him get angry and stomp off, swearing loudly as he went. Pete was about 5 ft. 9" tall, stocky build, grubby hair and full face. He was usually wearing a dirty, old gray baseball uniform, cap and all. He loved to fish and drink beer, not necessarily in that order, and he was good at both of them.

There was another character in town that I never had the occasion to meet. They called him "Indian Joe". My friends kept telling me stories about him but he may have been just a mythical character because as a person he never physically materialized anywhere. Joe supposedly had buried some gold up in the hills on the northwest end of town. People searched for years for his "stash" of gold but it was never found. I didn't really believe the story so none of my precious time was spent looking for it.

Not long after we moved to Bellaire, we began to see two brothers pushing wheelbarrows along the roadside. One might think there was a road project close by but we soon realized that wasn't the case. These fellows were as goofy looking as their wheelbarrows, which were quite a sight to behold! Their "<u>wheels</u>" were all decked out with rear-view mirrors, raccoon tails, American flags and the like and painted numerous colors. The brothers were feeble-minded and just walked the roads as self-appointed road rangers ready to help anyone who might have a vehicle breakdown. I guess if you broke down and needed a ride to town, they would plop you in the wheelbarrow and tote you there. Although I never heard of anyone who had actually enjoyed that wonderful experience, they were quite proud of their "<u>wheels</u> " and willing to help anyone silly enough to take them up on their offers. It just so happened one afternoon, dad, on his way to town, had a flat tire (again). I swear, his whole life was fixing one flat tire after another. Anyway, who should happen along but "Frick and Frack". I don't remember their true names, but that's what dad called them. One of them approached dad and said, "I think you might have a flat tire"! "Would you like me to help you?" To which dad replied, "No thanks, I can handle it"! The lad then said, "It looks like it's only flat on the bottom side, so why don't you just turn it around a little bit and that will fix it". It was at least a week before dad could stop grinning about that one.

Neil Orcutt (I'm not sure about the spelling) was a funny little man who lived in Bellaire and I do mean "little". He was only about five foot tall but wore clothes and boots that were many sizes too big for him. Perhaps this was his way of compensating for his diminutive stature. Neil always wore bulky pants rolled up at the ankles, a long black coat that came down nearly to the ground and rolled up at the sleeves several times, a pair of huge, high rubber boots and a black cap. Because of his oversized clothes, he was quite a sight walking down the road. Neil was known around town as a **horticulturist** and there was nothing he didn't know about flowering plants. We had a huge flower garden that ran along the concrete walk from the side of our house all the way out to the street. Mother loved those flowers and it wasn't long before she met Neil and solicited his help. The two of them spent countless hours out there and mother paid him handsomely for his help. She was constantly praising him for his knowledge of plants and he worked for her all of the years we were in Bellaire.

Neil Orcutt

We soon learned that Neil had another great ability. "Roller-skating". Every Thursday night during the summer months, they would open the town hall at 7:30 for public roller- skating. There was music, colored lights, soft drinks and skate rentals. I was fortunate enough to have my own leather shoe skates but there were clamp-on skates for others less fortunate. Neil was one of those but could he skate! He would race around the floor bent over nearly touching the floor with his chin and his hands clasped behind his back to keep a low center of gravity. He was a "gas" to watch and the center of attention when he was on the floor.

During my high school years in Bellaire, I met a lot of good kids who lived in the area. It was a time after the 2nd world war when good things were happening and most families were thrilled to have their loved ones back home and enjoying the good life for a change. People left their homes unlocked, their keys in their cars and crime in the area was practically non-existent. I was fortunate to live there at that time and call some very good people my friends.

At the East end of town was a bait shop owned by the Rinckey family. Mother and father, two sons and a daughter! The boys were named Stub and Skeeter. Stub was my age and Skeeter a couple of years younger. Their older sister was a little on the wild side and added a little "spice" to life in the town. They all worked together as a single unit in the bait shop and provided a much- needed service to the town and especially the "resorters," as we called them. Stub and Skeeter were characters in their own right and were always doing something to make life interesting. Stub was old enough to drive (you could get your drivers license at age 14 in those days) and he owned a Model A Ford sedan. We all liked to roller skate and about once a week, we would take Stub's model A to the roller rink in Gaylord about 30 miles away. Once in a while their older sister would join us and play touchy-feely with me in the back seat on the return trip home. I was still a bit on the shy side and a little uncomfortable in the situation but figured it all played a part in my well- rounded education.

One winter Saturday afternoon I was driving dad's new 48 Hudson in town and when rounding the turn at the main intersection, here come Stub from the other way a little too fast for the slippery road and we collided in the middle of the intersection. (We hadn't planned to get together that day but just happened to run into each other). (pun intended!) Now I can't say whose fault it was because when I saw him trying to cut the corner I hit my brakes, which locked the front wheels and I slid right into him. It didn't do too much to Stub's Model A due to the thickness of the steel in the old car but it bent the Hudson up pretty bad. I thought my dad would be furious but he surprised me by simply saying, "well, son, this is your first one!" Unfortunately Stub's reckless driving would soon lead to his untimely demise.

The following summer, while driving alone heading out of town on North M-88, he attempted to pass a car that was making a left turn and Stub rammed him broadside! Stub was thrown thru the front windshield and broke his neck in the fall. Stub was well liked and the whole town came to his funeral. It was a sad time for Bellaire and all of us who cared for him. From that time on, the town wasn't the same for the lack of Stub and his superb, gregarious personality.

Frick and Frack

Chapter Five: Saturday Nights

When one mentions the phrase "Saturday Nights", everyone's thoughts go instantly to a particular time or incident of personal experience that generally evokes a smile of good times gone bye and that is certainly the case here. My memories of Bellaire on Saturday night were without exception of good times. In the mid 1940's, summertime Saturday nights were magical for all who came to town to participate in the small town experiences that evolved from just their being there and enjoying each other's company. There were dances, box socials, free movies, popcorn, and cotton candy vendors. People would just walk the streets, socialize with others, turn around and walk back the other way to do the same thing all over again.

The lakes in the area were lined with summer cottages and the "resorter" people who lived there would come to town to mix with the locals on Saturday night. Young boys would meet young girls they might have known from the previous summer or new ones who were there for the first time and little romances would pop up all over. The lucky ones were not chaperoned and snuck away to dark places where romance became more exciting as they allowed their raging hormones to become unleashed with sheer abandon. And if they were still lucky, they might not have to deal with the results of that abandon at a later time. That one possible eventuality always kept me in line. I was still quite shy, but I made sure that I would never, never, embarrass my parents by making a stupid mistake as a young teenager. My parents watched me like a hawk and constantly threatened me with instant doom if I ever strayed down the forbidden path. The fact of the matter was, I just never got lucky! Even though I was still quite shy with girls, if I had gotten the chance, to hell with the threats, my hormones would probably win out and send me to hell! My parents were especially cautious when Milt's daughter, Mary Lou was around. They were aware of the smoldering feelings we had for each other, so we never had five minutes alone without one of the parents breaking up our potential liaison. After all, our families were new in town, business owners that employed a lot of the townspeople, and couldn't afford a scandal that might screw things up, big time. Eventually, all of Milt's girls did sew their wild oats, but I, unfortunately, was not the beneficiary of any of it. Yes, Billy boy was always good! (At least most of the time). I played a lot of sports and took my frustrations out on the field of play. I played baseball, tennis, golf, basketball, and anything else that might come along. On occasion when I would come home fully flushed in the face from my sports activity, my mother would look at me and demand, "Billy, what have you been doing"? Although she never said it, I knew she thought I had been fragging some girl. Probably Mary Lou. Sadly, I would explain that I had just played 3 sets of tennis, or just pitched a nine-inning ball game and that kind of exertion does get your blood flowing.

My mother was good to me and I loved her dearly. She knew deep in her heart that I would never intentionally embarrass her. Mother was a good person and a pinnacle of the community. She belonged to the social and garden clubs in town and held a seat on the school board. We attended church every Sunday and lived up to our good reputations. Later in life, I regretted that I had lived such a sheltered life during those years. As a young virile male I sure missed a lot of "pune-tang" that was there for the taking!

My sister, Yvonne, on the other hand, wasn't quite as "lily-white" in her behavior. As a freshman in high school, she dated a senior and quickly got herself pregnant. Actually, of course, it wasn't <u>all her</u> fault. Her boyfriend, John, did have something to do with it. She was vulnerable and he took advantage. John did the honorable thing and married her before their first child was born. Their little girl, Diane, was the first of 6 children they were to have and John was a good guy and a hard worker. Unfortunately though, they were too young with too many responsibilities to further their education and they struggled financially all of their married life. John began to stray with other women early on and they finally divorced after about 30 years of marriage. My sister, bless her soul, had a pretty tough time. She suffered miserably with allergies and asthma her whole life and then succumbed to lung cancer at age 75. The strange thing about it is that she never smoked or drank nor did either of her two husbands. How she acquired the cancer remains a mystery to this day.

I said John was a hard worker and he was as long as the work was related to farming. He loved the farm life and they lived on farms the majority of their life together. Other laborious endeavors were of no interest to him, especially home maintenance! Yvonne would constantly complain that after working in the barn, John would come in the house for meals and leave his manure-clad shoes on his feet while eating. It's no wonder that Yvonne had bad allergies with having to clean up cow shit every day from the inside of her house. John refused to take off his shoes until he went to bed and her allergies had to sustain that all their married life.

When they were first married, John did not have a steady job. One day, to help them out financially, my parents offered him the job of painting our house instead of hiring a local painter to do it. The house needed painting and John needed money so he agreed and proceeded to begin from the top and work his way down. Our house was quite large and had dormer windows to the third story on both the north and south side. The dormers were accessed by the roof, which was covered with green shingles. He had to tote the white paint up a ladder to the green roof and then walk on the roof to the dormers. Simple enough, right? Well maybe, but not for John! He wasn't on the job for fifteen minutes when he slipped and spilled a whole gallon of white paint on that beautiful," green roof." Dad was mortified, no! He was pissed!, and that was the end of John's painting career. And guess who got the job of fixing the white paint on the Kelly green roof problem? Yep! You guessed it, "Billy Boy". I had to take a piece of shingle down to the hardware store and get some green paint to match the shingles and paint over them two or three times until it covered the white. I was only 13 years old at the time but I didn't spill paint! I think John did it on purpose. He didn't really want the job anyway. After that, my parents just gave them money when they needed it.

Chapter Six: Boats

My friend, Plug Head Allen, and I, loved to cruise up and down the river to fish. But after awhile, we decided the hand made boat of mine was too laborious against the river current and we craved having an easy paddling canoe. Neither Dave's mother, or my parents, felt the necessity of buying us one, so one day we decided to take the matter into our own hands. The thought never occurred to us to hire out as labor somewhere and earn the money to buy one. Besides, even if we did, it would take us too long and we needed it now! It just so happened that a canoe belonging to one of the prominent businessman in town was tied up on the river near Warner Bridge. Warner Bridge was the steel framed, two-lane bridge crossing the river on the Southwest side of town. The main highway running West from town there rose up a fairly steep hill after crossing the bridge and meandered through the hills about three miles to Torch Lake. Local town kids did a lot of swimming and diving off of Warner Bridge. From the top rail of the bridge to the water, was a distance of about 30 feet and the water there was only 6 to 8 feet deep so the divers had to be pretty skillful not to hit bottom and break their neck. To the best of my knowledge, no one was ever injured diving there. Considering the risk, that had to be some kind of miracle!

Anyway, Dave and I conjured up this plan to swipe the canoe. He would carefully take the canoe after dark one evening and let it drift about a mile down the river to a spot we had previously scoped out on our river front property and hide it up on the bank behind the bushes. I made Dave do the dirty deed because 'I was too chicken to do it myself! Keep in mind that except for about the first quarter mile down river from the bridge, there was nothing but dense woods on both sides of the river all the way to Lake Bellaire. After a couple of days when our little thievery was discovered and Dave was caught, he quickly implicated me as his partner in crime, and rightly so. Even though I didn't do the taking, I was equally involved in the scheme.

I don't know what we were thinking. There was no way we were going to enjoy using the canoe on the river without someone seeing us and spilling the beans. I guess no forethought is typical of teens seeking adventure without a care for the consequences. Thank heaven the owner was an understanding good man and a father himself. Not only did he not press charges, but told us we could use the canoe anytime we wished <u>as long as we asked permission first!</u> As I now recall, the main reason we were caught is because I stupidly confided in my friend Mary Lou, who told her parents, who told my parents about the same time that someone else saw us with the canoe. Dave and I were ceremoniously marched sheepishly to the owner's house where we blurted out our confession and apologies! It didn't turn out too bad though. Not only did we not have to go to jail and subsist on bread and water, but we learned a good lesson at an early age before we got involved in a life of crime.

Now in the eyes of Mary Lou's dad, I instantly became a <u>bad ass -delinquent</u> and he forbade Mary Lou and I to spend any time together. Time would prove him wrong though, because it wasn't me who became the troubled teenager, it was his own daughter. For some reason, unbeknownst to anyone else, she became a kleptomaniac and had to continually be bailed out of trouble. Mary Lou was a pretty gal, a real "looker" and went on to get a reputation as "easy" with some local men. Now there's a lesson for him! If he had let me be more pro-active in her informal education and spend time with her, I could have straightened her out, so to speak, and spared everyone all of that embarrassment and shit! Who's to know? Her older sister, Nan, was also a looker with a wild streak. But Nan never got in trouble and was smart enough to limit her wild side to one man whom she eventually married and to my knowledge, is still happily married to. Then there's the youngest girl, Sylvia. But that's another whole story of it's own!

Chapter Seven: The Fights

Late that first summer, Dave had a cousin come to visit him from Iron Mountain, Michigan in the U.P. Doug was a toughie! He was strong, had a great build and was a troublemaker. He hung with us and I knew immediately we were not going to hit it off. I was slightly taller than him but he thought he could intimidate me and tried to order me around like a gang boss to do his bidding. Doug didn't know it but I was the strong, silent type. I didn't build my muscles chopping wood and shoveling sand for nothing. I never went looking for a fight, but if it came to me, I never backed down! I had learned to box while still in the Detroit area and was unafraid of anyone who might challenge me.

One day, Doug met my sister at my house and later had the gall to ask me to set her up so he could take her into the woods and have his way with her. That was the wrong thing to ask of me! I absolutely refused and the fight was on!

We agreed to meet in the back alley behind the drug store at noon the next day and see who was the better man. Doug had a big ring on his right hand that he said he couldn't get off and I figured he would try to use it to bloody me up. In my eagerness to get on with it, I agreed to fight him with it on and it bloodied my lip slightly, but I gave him the beating of his life! He didn't know about my previous interest in boxing, and thought I would be a pushover. I had two sets of boxing gloves from the age of 10 with a punching bag, and did whatever I could to learn the sport. I hit Doug about 10 times before he could get his first swing in and cut him deeply above his right eye. When he realized he couldn't box with me he tried to wrestle me to the ground. We hit the ground but with my right arm under his chin and me on his back. I held him in a strangulation grip and slowly tightened it until he could hardly breathe and no longer struggle. He was bleeding profusely now and when he realized his condition was worsening, he gave in and I let him up to go find a doctor and get sewed up. That night I saw Doug for the last time at the skating rink where he appeared with a huge bandage over his eye. He said to me", as soon as I get this bandage off I'm coming after you". I replied simply, "I'll be waiting for you and the next time I'll bloody both of your eyes"! The next day he went back to Iron Mountain and I never saw him again.

Now, I was not a bully and my ferociousness as a fighter surprised everyone, especially, after the incident the following night. I had tied up my little hand made rowboat to the dock by the swimming hole at Richardi Park. There happened to be another big kid in town named Ray Grannis. He was two years ahead of me in school, about 2 inches taller and 40 pounds heavier. After my fight with Doug I guess he figured he could take me on so he found my tied up boat and proceeded to sink it to provoke me into a fight. He was right, I was provoked and I sought him out. Word got around and my friend, Mary Lou told me where I could find him the following night. About 8 P.M. Mary Lou and I trotted down to the bowling alley in town where Ray was bowling. I told her to go inside and tell him I wanted to talk to him outside. He came out and demanded, "what in the hell do you want?" I said calmly, "I heard you are the one who sank my boat, is that true?" Yes I am, he replied, and what are you going to do about it?" I didn't say another word but hit him square on the jaw and knocked him flat on his ass! He had the most surprised look on his face as he struggled to get up. As I prepared to hit him again, he pleaded with me, "Please, don't hit me again, I'll go bail your boat out and tie it up to the dock where it was"! I said, "fine, get your ass up there right now and do it." He did and I never had another problem with him or anyone else in town from that moment on! The word spread quickly that I was one kid not to be messed with!

The next day my father sought me out to have a "father to son talk". He asked me what was going on? I simply explained that people were taking advantage of my good nature so I decided to put a stop to it. He understood and that was the end of it. For all of the years I lived there I never had another confrontation with a bully.

Chapter Eight: The Kalkaska Movie Experience

Back then, Bellaire and the whole area around it was as beautiful as a storybook! Not only in the summertime when magical things happened, but in wintertime as well. During that first winter, before we had a movie theatre in Bellaire, my parents and the Semrau's decided to go to the movies one Sunday evening at Kalkaska, about 22 miles away and I went with them. It was a very pretty but cold, clear, evening with deep snow on the ground and an absolutely gorgeous sunset! The multiple hues of pink, orange, blue and purple changed constantly as they danced across the western sky. Snow crunched under the car tires as we rode along silently, admiring the view, towards the small town of Kalkaska. If you have ever experienced this in the winter- time there, you know what an enchanting thing of beauty it can be.

The theatre was small but with fairly comfortable seats. It was toasty warm in there and we all settled in to watch the classic movie "How Green is My Valley". It was a mesmerizing movie that kept your complete attention from one scene to the next and we were all entranced until <u>suddenly</u> a whiff of a somewhat different odor drifted over us like a cloud and shook us back to our senses, especially our sense of smell! Some old bean -eating farmer in the audience had lost control of his sphincter muscle and farted us all into oblivion!<u> Now this was the mother of all farts!</u> It could peel paint off of the wall, make the fillings fall out of your teeth, it would open the eyes of dead people and take the gold metal at the <u>Fart Olympics</u>!

We all looked at each other disbelievingly but didn't know what to do about it. I wanted to stand up and start pointing fingers but quickly decided against that drastic tactic. Should we all bolt from our seats coughing and flailing our arms wildly as if trying to escape from a swarm of bees, or should we just sit there holding our breath and suffocate silently in the stink until it passes? <u>If it passes?</u>

Remember now, we were not in an outdoor theatre or an air- conditioned one either. We were in a small, warm, closed room with a bunch of strangers all suffering the same dilemma! No one in our group moved so I froze and we all just sat there and suffered silently for what seemed to be an eternity. Finally, as the air began to clear and we could see the screen again, "pfffffffffft!" he did it again! "Now this was the fart that broke the camel's back"! and the theatre began to empty quickly. There were cries of "Oh my God" "not again" and "who in the hell is doing that?" "That's enough" and "Let's get out of here!" It was almost a stampede! I rose from my seat and looked at my parents for direction, but they all just sat there with big smiles on their faces. My God, I thought, was it one of them? My dad said, "sit down!" "we drove 22 miles to see this movie and no foul farting farmer is going to chase us out!" "Holy man!" I could have done without that part of my education! If this was a lesson in life, I'm not quite sure what I learned. Perhaps it was patience. Patience, under the worst possible conditions! OK! It had to be that. At least there was a lot more elbow- room for the rest of the movie and evidently the guilty one couldn't stand it either. He must have left with the others, because eventually the air was clear for the balance of the show. I guess there is just no telling what some people will do to teach others a lesson!

Chapter Nine: The fireplace

Mother always wanted a fireplace. But before I finish this story, the previous statement reminds me of a little episode that many of my extended family will never forget. My first wife, Sally, had an uncle Harry that was unfortunate enough to contract cancer and passed away in his 70's. Because he was a veteran he was given a military funeral complete with a seven-gun salute. The old veterans dressed in their military uniforms did their best to carry out the salute but some of them hadn't fired a gun in many years and that part of the ceremony was a little rusty. At the command of " Ready, Aim, Fire"! Some of the old boys were a little slow in pulling the trigger and others were visibly rocked by the recoil of their weapons and struggled keep standing! As you can imagine, the result was an inconsistent spattering of gunfire and stumbling to regain footing after the fact. It was too humorous to keep composure without laughing. Everyone attempted to muffle their laughter by hiding their faces in their hands or turning around the other way. But that was nothing compared to the incident during the following wake. Sally and I and our sister-in-law were sitting across the table from the deceased's wife, aunt Mabel. Mabel was a nice lady but not well educated. Pleasant discussion was taking place when dear old aunt Mabel said. "Wasn't the ceremony beautiful?" Harry always wanted a "firing squad"! Now you know why I had to digress just a little from my fireplace story!

As I was saying, mother always wanted a fireplace, so after the foundation wall was replaced, from the digging of the basement, dad decided to build one on that wall. It just so happened there was an excellent stone- mason in town by the name of Steve Shippey. Steve was in his mid fifties and quite a character himself. I think that little towns have more characters per capita than larger cities. At least it seemed that way to me. I never knew any "characters" in St. Clair Shores, but I suppose they had their share. Steve had a good sense of humor and always had a joke to tell if you had time to listen. Dad sought him out, showed him what he wanted and they agreed on a price for a Michigan cut-stone fireplace that would rise on the West side of the house over three stories tall. The first thing they had to do was to pour a huge, deep concrete slab at the site to carry the tremendous weight of it all. The fireplace was about six feet wide at the base and had to rise about forty feet to clear the peak of the roof sufficiently for proper airflow. The fact that it was cut-stone of course added to the difficulty and henceforth to the price, and took Steve's crew several weeks to complete. I don't know how much dad paid Steve to construct it, but in today's dollars it would run at least $50,000. Today, some 60 years later, it still stands, beautiful as ever and a testament to Steve Shippey's abilities. During that first winter of 1945-1946, we kept toasty warm from the many cords of wood burned in that fireplace, including wood from the old barn that had stood behind the house.

Chapter Ten: The Hunt

Fall was approaching now and I was thrilled with the prospect of hunting. Whenever I could find a Field & Stream magazine, I would read it from cover to cover and couldn't wait for a chance to experience some of the stories in that magazine. Unfortunately for me, I would have to find someone to hunt with because I was still too young to get a license. My uncle Merle had given me a 22 calibre semi-automatic rifle and I was anxious to try it out. One of the requirements for an under age person to obtain a license was to attend a gun school put on by the local conservation dept. I attended the school with my 22 and in no time had mastered the nomenclature of the gun as well as the many safety rules for carrying and firing it.

Dad was not the least bit interested in hunting and it took a lot of coaxing and assistance from my mother to finally persuade him to go deer hunting with me early one

Saturday morning. We drove out into the country slowly down dirt roads until I spotted a herd of deer in an apple orchard about 300 yards from the road. I had my 22 rifle but the only gun dad had was a 38 police special hand gun he had purchased when he was a deputy sheriff for a short while back in St. Clair Shores. Dad said, "go around behind them and drive them towards me." Knowing dad, I should have been suspicious of that plan to begin with but my anxiety to get going overcame the suspicion. Dad said, "creep up on them and see if you can get a good shot and if not perhaps I can get one". I replied, "OK" and started out. My heart was pounding in my chest with the thrill of the hunt and although it was bitter cold out with about a foot of snow on the ground, I would have gladly crawled 10 miles on my belly to be able to come home with a trophy buck. Wouldn't mother be proud of me! I started out but It took me a good thirty minutes to make my maneuver until finally, I peeked over the top of the hill just in time to see their white tails bobbing in the breeze about 100 yards away right in the direction of dad's car. What a disappointment but at least dad would get a shot and put some meat on the table. I waited and waited but no shot! What happened to dad? There were at least two sets of antlers I could see as they ran from me but they were too far for an accurate shot with my small caliber rifle. The deer disappeared over a hill and I walked swiftly back to the car. As I approached it, I couldn't see dad at all. What could have happened to him? I opened the car door and there he was, flat on his back in the rear seat, sound asleep and snoring loudly. I was pissed! Angry, and disappointed! I woke him up and he could see the disappointment in my eyes. I couldn't say much to him because he was a strict disciplinarian and I didn't want to make matters worse. Dad kept me on a short leash. I said "didn't you see the deer? Why didn't you shoot?" He grunted something unintelligible with a sheepish look on his face and drove us silently home. That was the first and last time I would ever go hunting with him. So much for doing things with my dad!

It has been many years since I have lived there, but as I remember it, Bellaire in winter was just as enchanting and beautiful as it was in the summer. It snowed nearly every day between the middle of November and the end of March and the accumulation was so deep, there was very little road traffic. Commerce slowed and many businesses just closed up for the winter months because of a lack of tourism. This, of course, was before the days of Shanty Creek Resort and the influx of skiers. Most people just hunkered down at home or ventured out from time to time to visit close neighbors and friends. We had many "snow days" from school back then due to the inability of the snow- plows to keep the roads open to for the school busses.

One weekend morning after an all night snowfall, my brother Bud and I decided to take our two- runner sled out to the hills behind the school for a little fun. The school was only two blocks from home and that particular hill was quite steep from being chopped down to accommodate the grade school building and playground. We figured it would make for a speedy downhill thrill! Snow was still falling gently and it was very quiet. What a gorgeous scene with the snow piled high on the tree branches. Every thing pure white and still and as we left the house, a lone deer stood in the middle of the road just a block away. He gazed at us for a moment, and then slowly walked down the middle of the road toward town undisturbed by either man or his foibles. Nothing else was stirring except my brother and I that early Saturday morning, so I guess he was going to just take a tour of the town.

Within minutes we were at the top of the hill. Now you must understand that my brother Bud and I were sledding novices. Back in Detroit there were no hills to slide down. The ground was flat and to get a ride on a sled, one of us had to pull the other. We didn't live close to a park so there was no place to ride on a sled except in the driveway. Our sledding jaunts were brief and our experience nil, so we decided to slide down this here hill lying face down on the sled. You see, we wanted to be as close to the ground as possible just in case something happened and we had to bail out. We weren't stupid you know! I being the bigger of the two would lay face down on the sled and Bud would lie on my back. As we eased the sled over the top edge, we were all smiles in anticipation of the thrill we were about to experience on a fast, fun ride. <u>Well, --- not exactly!</u> What we didn't know, but were just about to find out, is that hill was not grassy underneath the snow but all unfrozen gravel. The steel runners on the sled cut right through the four inches of light snow with a lurch and launched us face first, tumbling ass over applecart like a couple of rag dolls until we hit the bottom with our faces down in the dirt and our mouths full of gravel! "Yet another lesson in our education of life in northern Michigan!" We were a sorry sight as we came home dragging that sled and our gravely asses behind us. I think we both spat gravel for a whole week after that little experience. <u>The big lesson – rail sleds are only good on ice and not on fluffy snow!</u>

The next time we went sledding it was with a toboggan so we could stay on top of the snow where we belonged. Just west of the school and about ¼ of a mile from our house, the hills got bigger and one of them was nearly bereft of trees on the northern slope. A new friend of ours, Ronnie Chapman, lived just across the street from the hill and he owned the toboggan. We spent many fun-filled winter days sledding with Ron on that slope. That is, until one fateful day when one single tree at the bottom of the slope got in the way. The hill was so steep and the sled so fast that it threw up a huge blur of snow in our faces coming down the hill. In the past we had managed to avoid the tree by taking a slightly different direction one side or the other but for some reason we misjudged it this time and were headed straight for it. There were four or five of us on the sled including Eloise Bachelder who loved the snow sports as we did and frequently joined us on our forays, and had we hit the tree it could have killed us all. Luckily, someone saw the tree through the blur of snow, yelled "bail," and we all tumbled off just in time. Needless to say, that was the end of the toboggan, but not the end of my winter thrill rides!

After my first summer in Bellaire, my best friend (Plug Head Allen) was forced to move down state with his mother and I rarely saw him again. When school started that fall, I met another boy by the name of Lyle Jensen who lived in town over the drug store. His parents owned the store and Lyle and I struck up a good friendship that lasted not only the school years, but many thereafter. Lyle and I both took shop class during our freshman year and we came across the idea to build a bobsled. We didn't have much money to buy parts but there was an old dump in town that we picked through to find old buggy wheels with steel runners. The steel on those old wheels was malleable enough for us to use as the bobsled runners. Hardwood was too expensive for our pocketbooks so we decided to make the sled and runners out of white pine including the side support rails.

Directly on the west side of town there is a steep hill running up from the river- bed and there are several streets that run up the hills lined with houses on either side. All of the streets dead- end about half way up the hill but one of them had an open pathway extending all of the way up to the town reservoir on the top. The Intermediate river meandered from the northeast end of town to the southwest end and then on down another mile and a half to Lake Bellaire. The terrace road, (Genesee St.) as it was called, ran south from the school about 50 ft above the river to Bellaire Highway on the south end of town west of Warner Bridge. There were several homes built atop the embankment on both sides of the terrace road and from the top of the reservoir down to the terrace was a distance of about 1000 ft. After we had built our shiny new red bobsled, Lyle and I figured if we started at the reservoir, we could steer the sled carefully down the path and then if we could navigate the bump at the end of the path, <u>we would have one hell of a ride! Little did we know what a ride that would be!</u> You know, when you are young, you feel indestructible and do things older people would never think of doing. So we were adventurous, unafraid of potential dangers and laughingly said to each other, "let's give it a go!" We solicited the help of my brother Bud to stand at the bottom of the hill at Terrace road to let us know when no cars were coming and then dragged the sled up to the reservoir at the top of the hill and waited for the "ALL CLEAR" signal. It was just a couple of minutes when the signal came and we climbed on the sled and began our highly anticipated, exhilarating journey! Now I want to tell you, that sled was <u>fast!</u> So fast it was nearly impossible to control. The ass end of it had a mind of it's own and kept wanting to take over the lead but somehow we recovered and kept it on a fairly straight line as we zipped at "breakneck" speed down the icy hill! About halfway down we hit a couple of bumps and the sled turned sideways, then as soon as it straightened out we hit another big bump, the side rails broke off in our hands, and we both went airborne <u>without the sled!</u> Some distance later, <u>we landed on our asses</u> and slid that way for about 200 feet down that icy road as the sled shot past us, crossed over Terrace road and took to the skies over the embankment on the far side! A couple of seconds later we heard it crash into some trees down by the river and break into a hundred pieces!

It had taken us about two months to build that damn sled and only one ride to demolish it. So What! we didn't get hurt. We laughed about it and both agreed the brief, thrilling ride was worth it All!

Lyle got a lot of experience sliding on his ass that winter. One morning as I was walking up the hill to school, Ronnie Chapman drove by me in his parents 1941 Ford coupe. Ron was a little guy and he could barely see over the steering wheel so I could only see the top half of his head. I took a second look and noticed Lyle was riding in the passenger seat as they drove up the hill. When they got in front of the school, Ron stupidly spun the car around on the snow-covered road just to show off his driving skills. As the car spun around, Lyle's door flew open and he came flying out still in a sitting position holding his schoolbooks in his lap. He landed on his ass again and slid across the road still gripping his books with both hands. It was a hilarious sight with Lyle sliding and only the top of Ron's head visible as his hands were flailing at the wheel trying to control the spinning car. They were both the butt of everyone's jokes for a couple of days afterwards. Lyle's butt sliding antics were always breaking me up!

Lyle and Bill's first (and last) bobsled ride

Chapter Eleven: Resorts

Bellaire was a resort town, small and quiet in the winter, but booming in the summer time. Lake Bellaire, at the South end of the Intermediate River, encompassed some 1200 acres and emptied into Grass River at the south end of the lake. There were numerous summer cottages on the lake and a few small resorts. One of these, a resort named "North Arms", was located about a mile and a half west of town on Bellaire highway and on the north shore of the lake. It was a private resort owned by several wealthy families of down state origin and who brought their own black maids up with them to take care of their needs for the summer.

There weren't many blacks in northern Michigan back then and Bellaire had only one at the time, a single man named Raymond Evans. Ray did odd farming jobs for a living and everybody loved him. He lived on the north end of town and every day would hitch up his team of work horses to his 4 wheeled wagon and come down through town smiling and waving to everyone he passed. Ray had a big, toothy grin and as a single man, he would spend his summer weekend nights with the black maids at North Arms Resort. He would drive that rig of his down through town and then west over Warner Bridge out to the resort. Everyone always knew when Ray was "going-a-courting" because he would stand in his wagon all dressed up in his dark blue suit and big yellow tie, waving, smiling and yelling "hello" to everyone he saw. Sadly, one day a few years later, neighbors found him dead on the floor of his home. He had succumbed to a heart attack and died alone. The whole town went to Ray's funeral.

On the east side of Lake Bellaire was another resort. The main building was a huge, rustic log structure with several small cottages in the conclave around it. "Fisherman's Paradise" was well known for several states around and was owned by the Bechtold family in Bellaire. It had been built before there were good roads to the area and was accessed from downstate by the C&O railroad that ran right by it. A huge birch-bark canoe hung from the ceiling of the lengthy front porch facing the lake. It was a truly enchanting place and I was always in awe of it. Many of the townspeople worked there in the summer, cleaning cottages, cooking and keeping up the grounds. I even worked there for a short period one summer. Many years later I tried to purchase it but lost my bid to the State of Michigan who turned it into a park. I wanted to renovate it and turn it back to its glory days but it just wasn't to be. There were many good stories associated with Fisherman's but all I heard were bits and pieces of some of them so I don't feel qualified to elaborate further.

As you travel west from Bellaire on highway 620 about three miles, the road comes over a hill and makes an abrupt left turn at Torch lake. History has it that Torch is the eighth most beautiful inland lake in the world and if you view it from that hill on a clear summer morning, you would never doubt that claim. It is eighteen miles long, two to three miles wide and so purely fed with spring water, you could see through the several hues of azure blue and green to the bottom of the lake in over 50 feet of water. As it gets deeper, the blues darken to several hundred feet and it is truly a spectacular site. Torch is where the wealthy spent their summer and holidays. Interspersed with the elaborate cottages along the eastern shore were a few resorts. On summer weekends, little Bellaire was flush with "resorters" from the lakes who perused the shops, strolled the sidewalks and enjoyed Bellaire's Richardi Park with it's tennis court and small sandy beach situated on the Intermediate (Bellaire) pond and spillway.

Ronnie Chapman delivering Lyle to school

Chapter Twelve:
Richardi Park & Pond

The surrounding area of the quaint little town of 1100 plus people suddenly mushrooms to several thousand in the summertime counting the vacationers and tourists. The C&O railroad ran north and south through town with it's railroad bridge that crossed the river pond just east of Richardi Park and the power plant. Trains only ran twice a day so the bridge provided a great place to angle for pan fish upstream of the spillway.

The river there teemed with Rock Bass, Perch and Bluegill and mother encouraged me to take advantage of that so she could have a continuous supply of fresh fish for summer dinners. I loved to fish and competed with old hermit Parks for the best catch of the day. He was always out there on the pond and sometimes I thought that he had the best life in the world. I guess it didn't occur to me at the time that he was there as a necessity for his living and may have resented my taking from his fish pool. I looked at it as he was doing just what he wanted to do and chose not have to work for a living. He loved the wild animals around him and treated them as equals so that in turn they trusted him and were never in fear of him doing them any harm. His life there was completely compatible with nature.

Years later, after I had gone back to the big town to earn my fortune and give it back to those smarter than me, I returned to Bellaire with my family in order to raise my children in the kind, friendly environment I had been raised in. It wasn't the same, of course, but it hadn't changed all that much.

I had this desire to try and help the town return to the period I had so enjoyed so much in my youth. One of the first things I did was to rehabilitate the old tennis court. It had been neglected for many years and its' condition actually defied anyone to attempt to play tennis on it. The net was sagging and full of holes and there was no fencing around the court so every ball that was hit had to eventually be chased down somewhere in the park.

I approached the town council for funds to provide the net and fencing and volunteered to do the labor myself. The council heard me out and in its' infinite wisdom, made me a proposition! Since none of them were tennis players, I had to explain the reason for the necessity of fencing, painting the lines, and nets without holes. They told me they would provide matching funds for whatever monies I could raise on my own up to the maximum needed for the rehab. Now I enjoyed this! I had something I could sink my teeth into and I loved a challenge. I am sure they figured that was the last they would see of me and they had solved the problem without any cost or hard feelings from anyone. But if that is what they truly thought, they were wrong!

Even though I had been gone for many years, I still had a lot of friends in town and some of them were local businessmen. I first approached my old friend, Ordie Hierlihy who was now one of the owners of Vacationland Homes with his father. The Hierlihys were good, honest, community minded people and agreed to help with a nice donation. A few more calls and I had the necessary money for our half of the challenge. I attended the next council meeting with my deposit stubs as proof of my endeavors and took them by surprise. They were absolutely dumbfounded with my success! After a short discussion, they made good on their promise and agreed to provide the matching funds.

With the help of my brother, Bud, we painted the surface of the court and the lines, then supervised the installation of the fencing and the new net. In time we discovered that what we had accomplished was not so much the simple rehab of a tennis court, but the resurrection of community pride. You see, this was just the first step in the complete reconditioning of Richardi Park with all of the amenities as you see it now. After that one simple act, many others including the Bellaire Lions Club got involved and that feeling of community pride welled up in the hearts of the whole town. From one small seed, planted in the proper spot, a whole new tree can grow!

Chapter Thirteen: Baseball

Springtime in Bellaire was exiting for me. Not like the Detroit area where it was usually sloppy and muddy with overcast skies. The soil conditions around Detroit were deeply impregnated with clay that made things quite miserable until the temperature rose sufficiently to draw the frost out of the ground and dry out the mud. In Bellaire, the soil was sandy so when the snow melted, there was no mud or frost upheaval. Flowers sprang up through the snow on the south side of the houses and sunny days were almost always the norm. It seemed like the rain came mostly at night and rarely affected my outdoor sports activities, of which I had many. My parents made sure I had plenty of chores to keep me out of trouble during my idle times, not that I gravitated to trouble, but they didn't want to take any chances. I did a lot of wood chopping and grass mowing in our huge side yard. Power mowers hadn't been invented yet, or if they were, we were not aware of any on the market in town. So, push mower it was. Of course, the strong exercise was good for my health and muscle development during my growing spurt times and that would prove to be very beneficial to me over the next several years.

School ended for the summer on May 25th. The reasoning behind this is so the kids could assist their parents in the planting chores on their farms. Agriculture was the dominant source of income in those days as there were very few factories and tourism was still not that well established. The last day of school was a fun time for everybody. We were all bussed out to Craven Park east of town for games and prizes and it was at these games that an event occurred that would change my life and determine my future for the next several years. The event was a baseball- throwing contest! Even though I had just completed the eighth grade, my tall lanky body and superior arm strength enabled me to throw the ball over 300 feet in the air, further than any other boy in school by a good margin and it immediately caught the attention of the varsity baseball coach. I wasn't eligible to play varsity sports until the next spring during my freshman year, but he implored me to spend the summer months honing my skills and come out for the baseball team at that time.

On the east side of town on Broad St. was a large vacant lot where the town kids would get together on occasion for a pick-up baseball game about twice a week and that is where I spent a lot of my time when I wasn't fishing or chopping wood. My parents bought me a baseball mitt and catcher's mitt for my brother and bless him, he willfully helped me develop my pitching skills without complaint. I could throw the ball very hard and he absorbed a lot of punishment to his body from missed catches especially when I learned to throw a curve ball. I taught myself to throw a knuckle-ball curve that summer that broke so sharply it looked like it just fell off of a table, and Bud suffered a lot of bruises trying to catch it. But he stood in there for me and I was grateful to him for it. He didn't want to catch my fast- ball though because I threw it so hard and was pretty wild with it. I finally hit on the idea of using tennis balls for practice most of the time and that solved the problem. They didn't hurt so much.

My freshman and sophomore years on the ball team were not too eventful. We had late springs those years and only managed to play three or four games each season before school let out for the summer. The weather just did not lend itself to spring baseball in northern Michigan. I was, though, getting better and stronger each year and word spread through the tri-county area that there may be a baseball prodigy in the making.

In the spring of 1949, the weather warmed up early in April and this meant our schedule of 8 ball games (two per week) looked promising, providing we didn't get any rainouts. We lucked out and were able to play our whole schedule.

My catcher, Ordon Hierlihy, was a senior that year and I, a junior. Ordie didn't have a very strong arm but that was his only problem. He loved the game, as I did, and best of all, he could handle my sharp breaking curve ball. I had waited all winter long for this season and God had answered my prayers for good spring weather. Our first game was at Elk Rapids and I was really nervous. We were up to bat first and didn't score and now it was my turn on the mound. I walked the first batter on four pitches, then walked the 2nd and 3rd batters, loaded the bases and proceeded with 3 straight balls on the 4th batter. What a predicament!

I held the ball for a minute, stepped back from the rubber and looked to the heavens for help. I prayed silently and said, "please Lord, help me <u>now</u>." "I have waited so long for this moment and I believe in you!" <u>At that very moment, I experienced something that I cannot completely explain!</u> <u>A calmness</u> came over my body, my mind cleared and even though I was calm, I felt re-energized and felt I could accomplish anything I attempted. I reared back and threw a blazing fast- ball down the center of the plate for strike one. The 2nd pitch I started high and behind the batter's head. He ducked backward to avoid being hit and my curve ball broke sharply over the plate for strike two. I blazed the next pitch over the plate that he attempted to hit but the ball was in Ordie's mitt before he could get the bat off of his shoulder. Strike three and one out but the bases were still loaded. With amazing new confidence, I mowed the next two batters down on strikes, thereby striking out the side and we were out of the inning. From then on I struck out nearly every batter I faced and went on to pitch a no-hitter, winning the game 5 to 0!

Our 2nd game against Ellsworth was more of the same as I pitched another no-hitter. The third victim that spring was Central Lake. I was a little sloppy that day and walked a few batters but only gave up one hit. Our boys hit the ball well and we went on to win that one 7 to 2. The following game produced another no-hit triumph for me and our team went on to complete the entire 8 game season without a loss. Over all, I set a personal school record of giving up only 11 hits in 52 innings pitched with 118 strike-outs and no losses. It was the first time Bellaire had gone undefeated in the history of school sports.

And then the glory came! Reporters came from around the area to take my picture and write stories about me. I looked like a real hayseed in the pictures. We didn't have complete school uniforms, just old shirts that said Bellaire on them. I had purchased baseball pants from a store in Traverse City and had an old hat that came to a point on the top. It came off every time I threw a pitch and kept me busy retrieving it. Our school was small and did not have money for new uniforms. That was the way it was and it didn't bother me. I was caught up in the notoriety and glamour of it all, and unfortunately that was not a good thing!

In retrospect, I didn't realize it at the time, but it wasn't me who was the hero. It was the other players who backed me up and made the plays when they were needed. It was Ordie, my catcher, who did a fantastic job of blocking my errant and wild pitches, it was Fred Kent and Lyle Jensen, and Tom Marshall and Tim and Joe Conroy and Jim Mosier and all the rest of the team with a combined effort that resulted in that great championship season.

And above all, lest we all forget, it was the guiding hand of God that enabled it to happen. I don't want to sound like a preacher here! I try to live a normal Christian life but I am certainly not a preacher as you can tell by some of the passages in this book. But remember? Remember what happened in that first game of the season with Elk Rapids? When I looked up to the Heavens and prayed for God's help? He gave it! It was there, immediately! There is no other way to explain the transformation that came over me at that moment. And that was not the first, nor the last time he has been there for me. God has given me a guardian angel to look over me all of my life! There have been numerous times in my lifetime that I have escaped instant death without explanation, or money was provided when I needed it the most, or family and friend problems were miraculously resolved. All it took was prayer and the belief in the God I was praying to. The belief in God gives the believer another dimension that non-believers do not have! A believer can, when all else fails, give the problem to God and forget about it, and God will provide! I know, I am living proof of that amazing fact!

Getting back to that season and the things that followed. Scouts from all of the major league teams contacted me and at that time I could have signed with any of them and named my price. All I had to do was to forego my senior year in high school and it would have changed my whole life. After much thought and grinding about it, I chose to stay in school and get my high school diploma. This made my parents happy. They felt I was making the right choices in life and after all, if I wanted to play professional baseball, I could sign up after my senior year was finished, right? Well, not exactly!

Springtime in 1950 was miserable. It was cold, windy and snowy, just the opposite of the year before. We only managed to play 3 games and 2 of those in snowstorms. Because of the cold, I was never able to get my arm in shape and in one of the games, I dislocated my shoulder swinging at the ball. Luckily, I fell to the ground, landed on my shoulder and it snapped back into place. To add to my woes, my catcher, Ordie had graduated the year before and my new catcher, Tom Marshall, game as he was, was not able to catch my curve ball and ended up dropping the third strike on many occasions thus allowing the runner to beat it out to first base. The result was that many of those runners ended up scoring from the same scenario and we lost two of the three games. Poor Tom, he felt terrible about it and I felt badly for him. He was a good guy and not really cut out to be a catcher, but nobody else stepped up so he reluctantly took the job. From throwing in the cold weather, I developed a sore arm and couldn't throw a ball at all for two months after the season ended. Obviously, most of the major league teams lost contact with me except for the Detroit Tigers. I wasn't too concerned because they were the team I wanted to play for anyway. Because I had grown up in the Detroit area, I had always dreamed of playing for them someday and now I had my chance. Their scout, Schoolboy Rowe, understood my plight and told me to wait until my arm had healed sufficiently and then call him to set up my try-out at Briggs Stadium in Detroit. My parents had taken me to a couple of games there as a young boy where I had seen Hank Greenberg, Dick Wakefield and Hal Newhouser play and they were all my heroes.

Around the middle of June, warm weather had finally come to northern Michigan, my arm had healed and I was ready for a tryout. Schoolboy Rowe told me to bring my catcher, Ordie Hierlihy, with me if I so desired. I did and our two families had a thrilling trip to Briggs Stadium. They probably felt I would be more comfortable having my own catcher to throw to and I was pleased to have Ordie be a part of this with me.

It was a beautiful day in June when we arrived and the Tigers were playing Boston that afternoon after my scheduled tryout. The Tigers catcher then was Bob Swift and after I warmed up with Ordie, Bob took over the catching duties and asked me to show him "my stuff," with Schoolboy Rowe watching. All of this was taking place in the Tigers "bullpen" while some of the Tigers team members were taking batting practice on the field. Our parents were watching from the stands in the outfield and my brother Bud was taking advantage of the situation by gathering up all of the balls the players were hitting in the stands. By the time my tryout was over, he had amassed some 30 baseballs that he planned to take home with him! That, of course, wasn't to be. They gave him one ball but to his dismay, took the rest away from him.

Back in the bullpen, I was doing my thing. My arm was fresh, and I was fast! So fast that my pitches were rising and Bob Swift was having a hard time hanging onto the ball. Back then, radar guns weren't yet invented so there was no way to gauge the actual speed of my pitches. Bob was able to catch my curve ball OK though and both he and Schoolboy were greatly impressed with "my stuff". After the trial, Schoolboy told me to sit in their VIP box seat until the game was over and then come to his office to sign a contract.

I was ecstatic! This was the moment I had been waiting years for. After the game I rushed up to his office as quickly as my big feet would carry me. He had not arrived yet and the only one in the office was general manager, Johnnie McHale. What happened then was a complete reverse of fortune for me. Now there are certain phenomenon in life that are completely inexplicable and this one would once again change my life forever!

McHale had evidently been left out of the loop about my presence there that day and for some reason was not at all in a good mood . He asked me who I was and what I was doing there, and when I told him Schoolboy Rowe had asked me to meet him to sign a contract, he curtly replied. "Go home! We aren't signing anybody today!" And that was it! I was disappointed, and then I was angry! What the hell was going on here? Was this whole trip all for nothing? The longer I thought about it, the madder I became. I didn't say two words all the way back to Bellaire. Up to that point, I had been a celebrated young baseball prospect and now the air had gone out of my balloon. I was pissed and my ego had been badly damaged! An ego that had taken 4 years to develop had just been deflated in one swift "swoosh"!

It was a mistake, of course. The following week, I received a phone call from a very apologetic Schoolboy Rowe and he begged me to return to sign the contract. Unfortunately, my pride had been damaged beyond repair and I told him I would think about it and call him back. I never did.

Here is a life lesson and it took me many years to realize it. Pride is not necessarily a good thing, and too much of it can be sinful! It caused me to make a decision I have regretted most of my life. In retrospect, I believe it was God's way of punishing me for embracing it. I really wanted to play baseball for the Detroit Tigers, but I ended up preventing myself from realizing that dream.

Later on, during my junior year in college at Michigan State University, I penned a contract to play for the Chicago Cubs and played for two seasons in the minor leagues before meeting my first wife-to-be. But that's another story.

Chapter Fourteen: Nancy

Our third summer in Bellaire was beautiful. Actually, they were all beautiful for me, and very romantic times. This summer a new family had moved into town. Harry and Nina Anger were from the Detroit area where he had been in the trucking business. They had sold their business and somewhere learned that there was a need for a movie theatre in Bellaire and Harry wanted to do something less strenuous in his later years. They purchased a vacant lot on Bridge St. next to "The Grill" restaurant and proceeded to build the "Bellaire Theatre." That addition to our little town not only thrived, but had a positive effect on all of the other businesses in town, especially during the summer months when there were so many tourists in the area.

For me, it became especially great. The Angers had a daughter named Nancy and she was beautiful! She was a year younger than me and I was stricken as though I had been hit by a bus. I was instantly in love for the first time in my life and I adored everything about her. Nancy was tall and slender with dark brown hair and big, beautiful dark eyes. She had a smile that would melt a snowman at first glance!

I asked her for a date, she said yes, and that was the beginning of a storybook romance that would last until I went away to college in the fall of 1950. Nancy was a load of fun and though we usually went out with other couples, we liked the same things and were very compatible. I was quite fortunate that my parents had a new Hudson 4 door sedan that they let me use for dates nearly every time I asked for it. When dad bought the Hudson and brought it to town, it instantly drew a crowd of people to look at it. Hudson had a new streamlined design in 1948 and ours was the top of the line. There was so much room in the front seat, one passenger could sit on the left side of the driver or 4 could sit quite comfortably in the front seat alone. My buddy, Lyle Jensen also had access to his parents nice new Packard but they were reluctant to let him use it and rarely did. The Jensens were very conservative but always welcomed me into their home and store where I spent a lot of time with Lyle chatting at the soda fountain. I consumed a chocolate shake there almost every day but somehow never put on a pound of weight from it.

The Hudson became the "smooching machine" for Nancy and I and we had a lot of hot times in it, usually with Lyle and his girlfriend, "Gay Openo", in the back seat. Don't get me wrong though, as much as we would have liked to, no consummate sex ever took place there. We were certainly normal kids with raging hormones, but we were also well-behaved, good kids and very respectful to our parents. We would never think of doing anything that might embarrass them. Our parents knew that and trusted us, and that's why we were given the leeway we enjoyed.

Unfortunately, for me, this was a real conundrum. Nancy was my first real love and if I had it all to do over again, I am not so sure I would have handled it the way I did. If I had been more aggressive and had a full sexual relationship with her, we undoubtedly would have stayed together, gotten married, had children and lived happily ever after. I was heartbroken when we parted, but I guess it just wasn't meant to be.

Nancy was sweet, mild tempered and naive. I recall one incident when we were cuddled side by side on the couch in her living room with her parents looking at a sears catalog. As we leafed through it Nancy asked, "what is our state color?" We all thought for a moment but couldn't come up with it. I said, "why do you want to know?" She said, "I was looking at these sweaters I like and it says they come in red, blue, yellow, green, white, state color." We all started to laugh and she was embarrassed. It was moments like that, that deepened my love for her. Another time we were walking down the sidewalk towards town and I remarked jokingly, "Nancy, you walk like a country hick!" She said, "Well then, just call me country, or just call me c--- for short." I was instantly shocked that she would say that word, but then I realized she didn't know what it meant and I quickly just changed the subject.

I guess I was just as naïve as she was because I stuck my foot in my mouth one day when her parents were present. We were going to a dance and I went to pick her up. Upon my arrival at the door, there she stood in a beautiful new dress, smiling sweetly like she always did. Her parents were standing proudly behind her with big smiles on their faces and I blurted out, "Holy man, Nancy, you look good enough to eat!" Abruptly, their smiles turned to frowns and then back to smiles as they realized I meant like a cake or some other great food I liked, and not sexually.

We were a great couple in high school. Lyle and I were scoring stars on the basketball team and Nancy and Gay were cheerleaders. The four of us were always together. We double dated, played cards and always attended school functions together. With Lyle's parents owning the town drug store, Lyle worked behind the soda fountain regularly and we all spent many hours there on the swivel chairs, sipping cherry cokes and milk shakes. The girls didn't drink many shakes because they had to watch their figures but I didn't. At that age my energy was inexhaustible and kept me as lean as a racehorse, no matter how many chocolate shakes I consumed.

Chapter Fifteen:
Good friends

Another friend we had in town was Jack Matthews. His parents owned the Bellaire Funeral Home a block south of down town. Jack was a little on the pudgy side and not as good an athlete because of it. He was a sub on the team and eventually on the varsity football team in our senior year. We teased Jack a lot about his weight but he was a good sport and went along with it. He didn't really like to be the brunt of our jokes, it just seemed to come naturally to him.

One morning Jack was late for school and when he finally arrived, we asked him why he was late and he refused to tell us. His face got red and he just smiled and changed the subject. We knew something happened because he was a good student and was never late for school. Later on in the day, after persistent questioning, he finally broke down and told us what fate had befallen him. As he walked through town on his way to school he passed under a tree and a bird "crapped "on his head. So, obviously, he had to go home and take a shower before returning to school. He was too embarrassed to tell us right away, but finally realized the hilarity of the event and revealed it to his "buds". We all roared with laughter, including Jack and the event was added to his character resume.

After high school graduation, both Jack and I attended Michigan State University together and were dorm roommates for a couple of years. Jack was never much of a ladies man, but ended up marrying a nice girl whose wealthy parents owned a cottage on Torch Lake. Jack became a very successful insurance broker and spends his winters here in Florida. We get together from time to time and chuckle about the old days.

Another of my school buddies was Bill Crandall. Bill played center on our basketball team and was quite a character. The 3rd member of our "Big Three" had red hair and when he was embarrassed, he blushed the same color as his hair. He wasn't quite as tall as I so I would jump center on the tip-off and then he would play that position while I switched to forward. Quite often this would confuse our opponents for a while when they played man-to-man defense. Bill's left- handed pivot shot was nearly impossible to block and resulted in his being the team's 3rd leading scorer behind Lyle and I.

Bill wasn't very good looking but loved the girls. One might think his choices of the opposite sex were quite slim, but that wasn't the case. When we were seniors, he came to school one morning obviously distraught over something very personal. Even though I was one of his best friends, he wouldn't tell me what his problem was. Late that afternoon, when he and I were re-stocking the hallway soda machine, and were alone, he finally spilled the beans! He said, "I think I got Miss Green pregnant! What am I going to do?"

Now, Miss Green was the first Grade teacher at the school and she was a real beauty. At about 5'7" with long auburn hair, green eyes and a figure like a brick shit-house (as we used to say). All the good -looking young men in town including our basketball coach, Mr. Booth, were pursuing her. She was one of three newly hired teachers at school and was the best looking one by far. Why she chose to date Bill was a mystery to all of us. They kept the affair silent, although myself and Lyle knew about it, the rest of the townspeople, including my mother and her friends, thought she was "just the sweetest and purest thing" to set an example for the whole teaching staff. Ha! Were they naïve! As I said, several of us knew they were dating on the sly and we promised not to tell anyone about it. In this day and age, they would have carted her off to jail for sexual abuse on a student, even though she was only two years older than Bill. I said they were dating but to be truthful, all they were doing was screwing. She lived in town with a prominent and respectful widow lady, Edith Richards, who was a good friend of my mother. All the towns-people thought Miss Green was a pure young lady and an excellent teacher. Little did they know she had a secret, "wild-side." She was a good teacher. She loved children, hence her first grade teaching position and she may have secretly wanted to get pregnant.

Mary was only 21 years old and just out of Michigan State University. What was so ironic is that another of the new teachers was our basketball coach and he was crazy about her. Don Booth was a big, handsome guy and asked her to go out with him several times but she wouldn't give him a tumble. Bill was afraid that he would find out about them and boot him off of the team, but luckily, it never happened.

Bill had an old 1932 Ford model A coupe that he would drive to town after dark and park in the alley behind Edith Richard's house at a given time. Mary would tell Edith she was going for a walk and then sneak into Bill's model A and away they would go to some back road in the woods and "have at it".

Anyway, I did what I could to console Bill. He said he just got so carried away that he momentarily lost his senses and didn't use a rubber and was sure that he had knocked-her-up. As it turned out, she wasn't pregnant, she knew what she was doing, and avoided a pregnancy. It sure scared the hell out of Bill though. His parents were nice people and like me, he wouldn't do anything to embarrass them.

I was really envious of Bill that he was getting so much pune-tang and I wasn't getting any, but I wouldn't have traded places with him at that moment for a million dollars. Who needs that kind of stress anyway? Not me. A couple of years later though, maybe!

Another one of the young female teachers that came with the bunch was a fiery Italian redhead named Ann Romano who taught English and Home Economics. She told me once that I ought to aspire to be a writer because I had a talent for it! Ha! What did she know? This book is certain proof that she must have been out of her mind.

Ann and Mary Green were good friends and I think she knew about Mary and Bill's little tryst because all of a sudden she took more than a casual interest in me. My mother invited her over to our house for dinner one evening and she struck up a conversation with me about duck hunting. She knew I had a girlfriend, but in front of my parents, asked me to take her hunting the following Saturday. I was a little stunned as I glanced at my parents for support but they seemed to want me to do it, so I agreed.

At the break of dawn early Saturday morning, Ann met me at the dock under Warner Bridge where my boat was tied up and off we went drifting down the river. At that time of year, the middle of October, there is always fog on the river in the sun-lit morning and you have to be very quiet while drifting so as not to fore-warn the nesting ducks in the weeds on the river's edge before you can see them. At the slightest noise they will arise with a hell of a clatter of flapping wings and honking and if you had not seen them first, it would scare the crap out of you. I told this to Ann, but it evidently didn't matter to her because she chattered endlessly all the way down the river and then didn't understand why we didn't see any ducks. We didn't see any ducks because of her stupid yakking in the fog and I didn't get a shot!

Ole "one-duck Lovett" wasn't going to get one that day. Shortly, it became obvious to me that Ann's interest wasn't in the duck hunting at all, but in me! She wanted to get out of the boat and go into the woods somewhere along the river where there was a high spot so she could taste my youthful manhood and awaken her throbbing female passions! Well, I was young and horny but not that horny. She just wasn't my type and besides, I had to be loyal to Nancy, so after a couple of hours we motored back up the river, me duckless, and her passion still unfulfilled! She was obviously disappointed and I was pissed that I never had a shot to put meat on the table that night. We remained friends and I guess she got the message because she never came on to me again.

I find it quite interesting that back in those days, relationships between male students and female teachers were rare but acceptable when discovered, and no one went to jail or even worried about it. After all, young men were always horny and the chance to nail a teacher was something to be proud of and tell your friends about. I guarantee you, no psychological harm ever befell a male student lucky enough to have experienced it. If it happens now-a-days and it is discovered, all the do-gooders scream rape and the law prosecutes the poor, hapless female teacher for her natural participation. Let's face it, older women like young studs and young studs like the experience of older women!

"One Duck Lovett"

Although I didn't have a successful hunt with Ann Romano, she didn't either and eventually my duck hunting became lore in the little town of Bellaire. During the season, I would be on the river early in the morning before school and after school before basketball practice. They called me "One Duck Lovett" because I could only shoot one at a time. I had a single- barrel 12-gauge shotgun that kept me from re-loading fast enough before the rest of the ducks flew out of range. That one shot would scare all the ducks away within earshot and because I couldn't reload fast enough, that would be the end of it. As a result, I was always walking through town carrying one stupid duck. I didn't particularly like the taste of them anyway, but my parents did and I felt a sense of accomplishment for "providing for my family". As far as I was concerned, the best method of preparing them was to bake them in the oven on a wooden board, then throw away the duck and eat the board! I hunted only for The" thrill" of the hunt.

One day I went hunting after school as usual and I was a little late getting to basketball practice that was always held in the Bellaire Community Hall. Our school was old with a small gymnasium so all of our practices and games were held in the hall downtown. I rushed to the locker room to dress for practice and no one else was in the dressing room, so I knew I was late.

I quickly changed and ran up the stairs taking three at a time in huge bounds. When I got to the top of the stairs I was surprised to see all of the players sitting on the bleachers listening to then coach, Bill Boerner, giving one of his lectures. The door was open at the top of the stairway and as I came bounding up, I stubbed my toe on the top stair and went sprawling head first across the floor in front of the players and coach Boerner. I got a big round of applause and a lot of laughter for that little indelicate move. Was I embarrassed! Let's face it, at age 15 and 6' 3", most guys, including me, don't have very good coordination. It was so humorous, coach didn't punish me for being late for practice. I was thankful for that!

Chapter Sixteen:
Bellaire, The Town

Our little town was so unique. I guess most towns have their own little peculiarities related to the people who live there, but I doubt there are many with the distinct qualities of Bellaire. As little as it was, it was the county seat and therefore, the jail and courthouse were located in the middle of town. The Intermediate River runs thru it from the Northeast to the Southwest. Two road bridges and a railroad bridge span the river and provide locations for anglers to fish without the need for a boat. There were two bait shops in town and a hardware store to supply everything needed for a fishing- venture of any magnitude. The bait shops rented outboard motors and the one under Warner Bridge also rented boats or canoes. The town had two good doctors, one of which made house calls, a dentist and a barber-shop. So a body could get clipped from head to toe and for the good of the soul and there were also four churches. Catholic, Pentecostal, Methodist and later on a Lutheran church joined the mix. Two restaurants, a drug store, 4 gas stations and auto repair shops to keep the vehicles in shape and they were all kept busy thanks to the awkward driving of those who couldn't keep focused on the right side of the road for some reason or another. Of course, one of those reasons could be attributed to the local tavern with the usual percentage of tipsters who thought they could make it home simply by keeping it between the telephone poles.

We had three grocery stores of individual propriety that provided good food and service to all of their customers. After all, the day of chain stores hadn't been invented yet and everybody knew everybody else in town and what their business was. Gossip traveled quickly from one crank phone to another over open party lines and that kept the women busy and happy. What else could one ask for?

Even I, through my athletic abilities and hunting activities, had already gained minor celebrity status. And speaking of celebrities, the well-known and highly acclaimed water-colorist, Robert Culver, resided there. After his death at a very young age, he became nationally acclaimed and to this day, if you could purchase one of his paintings, you would be looking at shelling out thousands of dollars for that privilege. Bob lived in a small house above Warner

Bridge on the Southwest side of town overlooking the river and adjoining our own 260 acres of land.

Located in one of the downtown buildings was the local telephone office equipped with an old fashioned, plug-in telephone board system and a local operator. If you were one of the fortunate ones to have a phone in your home and you wanted to make a call, you would give the box a crank and "ring-up" the operator. She would say "operator" and you would tell her who you wanted to speak to. They tried to discourage the name thing, you were really supposed to know the other party's number, but if you forgot it, the operator always knew what the number was anyway. The numbers were like 26-R2 or 26-R4, depending on the number of rings it took to get that particular party because there were always up to 5 numbers on each phone line. If someone else on that line wanted to listen in on the phone conversation, all they had to do was carefully pick up their phone when it rang for someone else and listen in. The old busybodies in town loved that system and there was a lot of that that went on. I think there were only about 2 to 3 hundred phones in the entire system, hence the operator had them all memorized. Gossip is great in a small town. It is the juice that runs the machine, so-to-speak. In the cold winter months, when the snow is up to the telephone lines, hot gossip keeps the whole town running. It warms the souls of the gossip- mongers and eliminates boredom until the spring thaws. Finally, when spring comes, people can go out and do things to create more gossip to store away till the doldrums of the following winter cry out for it to blossom again!

Sorry about that! I just got carried away. Now where was I? Oh yeah, the town.

Bellaire also had a 5&10 cents store. Dalquists was the name and it remained there for several years until finally closing down in the 1970's after all the 5& dimes had run their course. There was a bakery in town and a small bowling alley located next to the bank at the corner of Broad and Bridge Street. Herb Bechtold, the local banker, was a conservative fellow and held the town in a tight fisted grip until his death. His brother, Vic Bechtold, was another town character. Being the town constable gave him an advantage because he was also the town queer. How about that conundrum? <u>The powerful banker who held the town in a tight grip and his brother, who got a grip on the townsmen whenever he could</u>. I guess I should be more politically correct and say he was "sexually challenged". A challenge he gladly met head on. Vic could usually be found walking the main streets in the afternoon and evening hours strolling along, slobbering on a big fat cigar. He was a bit overweight with his belly protruding from a long coat or rain slicker and sporting a crumpled old hat. Vic shared his house with a variety of young men from time to time.

I remember one especially humorous incident about Vic. A friend of mine, Fred Kent, had driven his old, lime green topless roadster to town and parked it next to the bank on Broad Street one evening while he went roller-skating in the Community Hall across the street. Fred was a great guy. He was physically short and a bit bow-legged but always smiling and would give you the shirt off of his back. He didn't have much in life but was one of those guys everyone liked because he was so even-tempered and had a great personality. This particular evening after the skating, Fred and I emerged from the hall immersed in a conversation about something or other and walked over to his parked car. There, lo and behold, stood constable Vic chewing on his big wet cigar with an irritated look on his face. Fred said, "oh- oh!" and he knew he was in trouble. Vic blurted out loudly, "I thought I told you to keep this pile of junk out of town until you got a license plate for it?" Fred scratched his head sheepishly and I really felt sorry for him. Finally he said, "I just don't have the money for the license yet." " Well, guess what! Said Vic. Don't you dare move that car until you get a license for it!" "It stays right there until it's licensed." Just then, our friend, Pete Wilks, came walking up with his shoe skates slung over his shoulder and inquired as to what the problem was. As Vic walked away, Fred filled him in, and said he didn't know what to do because he didn't have the money for the license plates. Now Pete didn't have much either. His mother was one of the town "ladies" and he did not know who his dad was. Pete did know how to work odd jobs for his meager spending money with which he had bought a nice pair of shoe skates and they were his pride and joy. We all knew that Pete had probably paid less for his skates than Fred had for that old car but Pete started to think and then said to Fred. "I tell you what, I'll trade you my skates for your car, even up!" Fred's car was pretty old and beat up and my God it was LIME GREEN! You could just see the wheels turning in Fred's head and with a big grin, he replied, "OK, it's a deal!" They shook hands, exchanged skates for keys, and that was it. That transaction surely has to make the record books somewhere! You have to remember, all Fred really had to do was to go home with Vic for a quick blow-job and his troubles would have been over and he could have kept his car. But, to Fred's credit, he was above that and I, for one, was proud of him. As much as I liked him as a friend anyway, I gained a lot of respect for Fred that day.

On the north side of the community Hall on Bridge St., was a variety store run by the Mosier family. Mr. Mosier was in ill health and passed away in 1955. Mrs. Mosier was a tall slender, nice looking lady in her late 30's or early 40's. They had a daughter and two sons. One about my age named Jim. After her husband passed, Mrs. Mosier and her children were left to run the store by themselves and it was no easy task for them. Jim was a year behind me in school and became a good buddy and palled around with Lyle Jensen and I.

The three of us played a lot of tennis together on the court at Richardi Park. We all became good tennis players and Lyle and I took on all comers in doubles matches. We took special glee in defeating the "resorters" who challenged us every summer. To the best of m y recollection, we never lost a match in doubles competition.

One day, Jim and I were playing a set or two with Lyle watching and waiting his turn to play the winner. Jim had saved his money and just purchased a new racquet that he liked the feel of. He had a bit of a temper and had developed a bad habit of throwing his racquet after losing a well played match or sometimes just losing a point and with his old racquet and it didn't matter much anyway because it had gotten pretty banged up along the way. On this day though, it was different. Jim had been very careful to control his temper. He did not want to damage this new racquet he had saved for so long to get. Although he was tempted several times, he caught himself just before giving it a big heave so Lyle and I congratulated him on his attention to self-control. While singing our praises to him, we couldn't help a little good-natured chiding as well. Jim was a good guy but also a little sensitive so our praises and chiding began to get to him as the match played out. On the last point of the match, which I won, Jim couldn't restrain himself any longer. He raised his arm high to fling the racquet as far as he could but at the last moment regained a modicum of control, lowered his arm, gave a little flick of the wrist and slid the racquet ever so slowly across the surface of the court for a short distance. The distance was small, the speed slow, but unfortunately, the aim was deadly as the neck hub of the racquet hit the net pole square on and broke it in two pieces. Jim didn't cry, after all he was a grown teen-ager, but he had such a pained look on his face, we thought he was certainly going to and as the smart-ass, cruel teen-agers we were, Lyle and I laughed openly at Jim's bad luck. Of course we felt bad afterwards, but we couldn't help reflecting on the irony of the whole incident. Old habits die hard, and even with good intentions they can come back to haunt you.

Vic Bechtold

Chapter Seventeen:
The Good Guys

Maybe it is just me, mellowing out in my old age, but as I recall those times years ago in the little magic town, I have nothing but good memories of the people there, especially my friends and acquaintances. There were a lot of good kids who lived there and I am sure their demeanor was largely attributed to the way they were raised by their parents, but we just didn't get into trouble. Sure, there was the occasional exception, and when it happened, it was big news, but it rarely happened. There was a **murder** in the area one year, however, but it was directly attributed to excessive alcohol consumption and a domestic dispute. That combination can be deadly anytime and anywhere.

I had good friends like Stub and Skeeter Rinkey whose parents owned the bait store on the east end of town. They had an older sister named Norma Lou. Norma was a little on the wild side and rumor has it she gave the guys a pretty good ride. She was too old for me and though she gave me many come-on glances, I was afraid of her. I didn't care for aggressive girls! Stub owned an old Model A Ford sedan that he drove to the roller rink in Gaylord most every weekend and quite often I would make the thirty mile trek with him, Skeeter and Norma Lou.

One Saturday night on our return trip, Norma Lou wanted me to sit in the back seat with her and although leery, I agreed. As we rode on in the darkness, she took my right arm, wrapped it around her, placed my hand firmly on her right boob and snuggled close to me. I was so scared I thought my heart would leap out of my chest! That may sound stupid to most guys, but I was barely 14 and not yet ready for that part of my education. I didn't know what to do. Norma Lou was 18 or 19 and obviously knew what she was doing and probably thought she would advance my sexual education right then and there. I thought to myself, should I squeeze her tit, and if I did, would I get slapped or would she just jump on me and go to it with her brothers in the front seat? **That would surely catapult me into manhood in a matter of minutes!** I froze! I turned to pale white stone and couldn't move a muscle. After about ten minutes of sitting with this stone, Norma Lou opened her eyes and said to Stub, "stop the car, I need to pee!" As she started to get out of the car, she whispered to me, "Want to come with me?" My throat was dry, but I managed to gulp out, "no thanks, I'll stay here." So out she went, dropped her drawers and relieved herself. I'm sure she expected me to peek at her, but gentleman that I was, I didn't.

Afterward I thought what a coward I was! I should have kicked myself a hundred times. I could have gotten laid for the first time or at least set up a future rendezvous for fun and games. She offered it up and I didn't have the guts to take advantage of it. I guess the truth of the matter was, I wasn't attracted to her and my fantasies only included certain other girls that I knew. Besides, her brother Stub was a good guy and I wouldn't do that with his sister out of respect for him. Unfortunately, Stub didn't live very long. Like most teenagers, he liked speed and although he only had this old Ford Model -A, he pushed it to the limit whenever he could and it would lead to his early demise.

Stub was heading north out of town on Bridge St. one afternoon with his usual heavy foot. He attempted to pass another slow-moving car driven by an old man who didn't see Stub coming up behind him and abruptly made a left turn into Stub's path. The Model A side-swiped the old man's car, Stub lost control and went end for end, throwing him through the windshield and breaking his neck! That was a sad day for Bellaire. Stub's funeral was one of the biggest the town ever had.

There was another kid in town by the name of Fred Smith. He lived on the north end of town close to me and was always doing something <u>devilish</u>! I first met him at the Methodist church in Sunday-School class shortly after we moved to Bellaire. The class was being conducted by Dr. Rodgers, the prominent town physician. Doc was a good man, a good doctor and would later play a very important role in my life. The good doctor stepped out of the classroom for a minute and Fred said, "see- ya" with a big smile on his face, opened the window, climbed out onto the dormer roof and was gone! When Doc returned, he could see by the looks on our faces that something was a-miss. He quickly gazed around the room and asked, "where is Fred?" We all pointed to the open window and Doc said. "That stinker, but I'm not surprised, this isn't the first time he's done that." As time went on, every time someone pulled a prank in school or around town, it was a pretty good bet that Fred had something to do with it. He never got into serious trouble with the law. He was just a fun-loving guy and practical joker.

Then there was Bill Hannan. A handsome, red-haired Irish kid a couple of years older than I. He loved to chase the girls and quite often took me with him. My parents didn't like him, I guess they thought he was a bad influence on me (duh!) One night after a particular late escapade, when we didn't get home until about 3AM, my parents found out and forbade me to go with him anymore. Rumor has it that he got his own "loving" anytime he wanted it with a girl who lived in a big farm house in the country. She was a senior when I was a sophomore and one of her best friends was a gal named Irene Koutnik. Irene lived in the country east of Bellaire and she was a real sexy thang! She took a liking to me and was determined to turn me into a red-blooded man forthwith! While double dating one night, Irene and I were riding in the back seat snuggling and smooching. She took my hand, opened my palm and rubbed her two forefingers back and forth across it while looking deeply into my eyes. Young kids nowadays probably have no idea what that meant, but back then, everybody knew the full meaning of the gesture. It meant, "I want you! Now!" I really liked Irene and even though she was a couple of years older than me, I was ready! Obviously, that was not the time or place for it, but I certainly got the message. My memory fails me as to exactly what happened later, all I remember is that for some reason, it didn't happen, then or ever. I probably just got cold feet and shortly after that I started dating Nancy Anger, the new love in my life.

About that time, before Nancy came along, I made another good friend while skating at the Bellaire Community Hall. Herbie Nothsdine had just gotten out of the army. He lived in Mancelona about 12 miles to the east of Bellaire and he loved roller-skating as much as I did. Roller- skating was one of the few activities where young people could meet each other without negative influences like alcohol or just carousing the streets. Kids and young adults would come from several towns around to skate and meet each other in a clean, risk-free environment. Herb was always there on skate nights. He was an excellent skater and we quickly became good friends. We both liked to skate backwards and do spins and jumps in the middle of the floor. Skate dances were also favorites of ours and because of our ability we always had plenty of girls wanting to dance with us. As a result, we usually each had a pretty girl to take home afterwards. Herbie also drove a Model A Ford sedan that we would take out to the park or country road and do some heavy "smooching". I must explain here that none of the smooching we did during that time resulted in aggressive sexual behavior. Some petting, yes, but we were all just experimenting and feeling our way a little bit. Like myself, Herbie was raised well, a gentleman with women and never pushed girls to "score". We didn't drink, so we never got ourselves into a situation because of stupidity. Herb and I thoroughly enjoyed each others company for a couple of years and the double dating always made it perfectly safe for the girls we dated. He eventually married and raised a family up there. I believe he also got into local politics and served his community very well for several years.

Chapter Eighteen:
Best Friends

When one is happy and living the good life, he has many friends, and conversely, when one is not happy, a good friend is nowhere to be found. They say if you have one good dependable friend in life, you are indeed, blessed. Well, my high school days in Bellaire were happy ones and I was blessed with a lot of friends. One in particular, I considered to be the best, and that one was Lyle Jensen. His parents owned the local drug store in town and Lyle was obligated to work there after school and on the weekends. His primary duty was to run the soda fountain and that was where I spent many hours on the other side of the counter drinking cherry cokes or chocolate milkshakes. I could down a big thick one every day and somehow never gain a pound. The secret of that, I'm sure, was my continuous rigorous exercise. Lyle and I played several sets of tennis at least every other day in good weather and when we weren't on the courts, we were shooting hoops in the alley behind his store, or we were playing baseball, or-r-r, we were rowing my boat up and down the river into Lake Bellaire and back.

During the cold weather, we played pick-up basketball games in the community hall. On top of that I did a lot of hunting and thus walking through the woods in the hills around Bellaire and on the river. I hunted Partridge, rabbits, squirrel, deer and ducks and never tired of the thrill of it. No wonder I stayed so slim and strong. Besides these activities there were other ways that Lyle and I left our mark on that magical little town.

In early summer of 1947 prior to our freshman year, we were pondering on how to earn some spending money for the summer without having to actually do much physical labor, which neither of us liked to do. I had enough of that already to acquire a natural aversion to it. Lyle remarked that his parents store received several catalogs from manufacturers and distributors wholesaling their products. His parent's drug store sold only a limited number of items unrelated to their business, so they had no interest in other things we might attempt to "market" with our own efforts, providing said items passed their <u>scrutiny test</u>!

So we poured through the numerous pages trying to find something we might be able to sell to our many friends and acquaintances in the community. We came upon t-shirts with team logo's and instantly realized our school's athletic teams had no mascot or logo of any kind. The teams were just called "Bellaire basketball or Bellaire baseball". (There were no other sports teams there back then). Our thinking was, if we could come up with a good mascot name we would initiate it as the team's logo, put it on t-shirts and sell them for a profit! We mulled over the names of several professional sports teams we knew and tried to associate ourselves with one that worked. We discarded the ones that we felt were over-aggressive such as Lions, Cougars or Bears and looked for something that was brave and gentle, yet strong. We didn't want to choose one that would appear as too passive to our competitors like Orioles or Cardinals as we felt they would give an impression as "sissies", so when we hit on the name "Eagles," we knew it was the perfect fit! Even though it was a bird, it was a proud, magnificent one and represented the feeling we wanted to portray. And that, ladies and gentlemen, is how the "Bellaire Eagles" got their name! We ordered a dozen shirts and sold them, then another dozen, and another dozen, etc. I can't remember why and when we stopped selling them. I'll have to ask Lyle. He and his wife, Gay still live in Hawaii but summer in Petoskey with their daughter, Jana.

When we began selling the shirts, we never thought of clearing the name with school officials or anyone else, for that matter. After all, we were the sports stars! Who was going to question us? (You see how a little fame breeds arrogance?) We simply chose the winged design and the lettering, "Bellaire Eagles" in red ink on the white t-shirts and began ordering. We borrowed the money for the 1st order from our parents and paid it off from our profits as the shirts were sold. We only added a $2.00 profit per shirt, $1.00 each for us, which gave us a little spending money for the summer season. <u>Now we had our start as salesmen and entrepreneurs!</u> It gave us confidence that we could accomplish something like that on our own so we decided to try another idea, why not?

On the property my parents owned west of town, stood and old apple orchard. It had not been maintained for years, but every fall, it was loaded with good- looking apples. Most of the trees were Northern Spies, an excellent eating apple and very popular in the area. Apparently, there were several other varieties in the orchard that we were unaware of because they all looked alike to us.

There were three grocery stores in town. Conners, Richards and Davies. So, like any good businessmen, we approached the owners and offered to sell them a few bushels of Northern Spies at wholesale prices. Old man Conners wasn't interested, so we went next door to Richards Grocery and made our pitch! At $10.00 per bushel, it was a hell of a deal for the grocers.

Both Richards and Davies jumped at it and we got orders for several bushels ASAP. Unfortunately, now we had to do some work. The apples wouldn't pick themselves so we set about to find some help and get it done. We recruited my little brother for a dollar a bushel and soon had filled our first order. We were careful not to pick the ones with worm-holes or marks and delivered them to the two stores.

In about a week, we went back to the stores and inquired about how sales were going. Mr. Richards was very pleased and said he could use three more bushels. Great! We could fill that order the next day and walked up the street to the Davies market to add to our previous order there. When we arrived at the store we noticed there were none of our apples on display so we assumed he had sold them all and would get another substantial order. As we approached the owner, Bob Davies, he had a grim look on his face and said, "come into the back room, I want to show you something!"

There in the back of the store were several bushels of rotten, stinking apples! "I thought you told me these were Northern Spies! They aren't, they are Wolf Rivers!" At that moment, Lyle and I got a quick lesson in apple horticulture and "Reverse entrepreneurship"! The Wolf River variety, although it looks a lot like a Spie, it is a larger, short lived, junk apple that is grown primarily to feed pigs and cattle. "I sold them as Spies" he said, "and my customers are very angry!" "Now what are you going to do about it?" Our jaws dropped, we were dumbfounded! We had already spent our profits and had no means of giving him a refund. Luckily, he said, "you know, it is not all your fault. I should have known the difference myself." "But no thank you, there will be no orders for more apples from you fellows!"

Boy! Did that take the wind out of our sails! One minute we were successful entrepreneurs and the next, we were failures and even worse, appeared to be "con-men"! Trying to pass off Wolf Rivers for Spies. Kind of a " bait-and-switch" mentality. Mr. Richards new order didn't get filled either because we didn't know one apple from the other to look at them and we certainly didn't want that humiliation again! Now we had a reputation in town as being con men, so we figured we had better go out of business for the rest of the year and that was the end of that money making partnership!

Chapter Nineteen: Dad and Bud

I have told you about my little brother, Arland, or Bud as we nicknamed him. He was the youngest and Dad's favorite with basically his same personality. Bud liked to get his hands dirty and do the more menial tasks while I liked to find the easier way to do things, using my brain wherever I could, instead of my brawn. Not that one method is superior to the other, it's just a matter of choice.

Dad had to take trips to the upper- peninsula and Canada in the company's stake bed-1934 Ford truck. In the early days of the log-cabin business he made the trips by himself to lumber cutters to purchase white cedar logs for the cabin mill. They used white cedar because it was more resistant to rot and more plentiful at that time. To this day, some 60 years later, there are still Bellaire Log Cabin cottages scattered around Bellaire and northern Michigan, a tribute to the durability of the wood and the finished product.

On one of these trips to the north in 1947, Bud went with Dad to keep him company. At the age of 10, he wasn't much physical help, but it was an adventure for him and someone for Dad to talk to, as the trip would normally take a couple of days. He would drive to the location, load up, sleep for 2 or 3 hours in the truck and drive back to Bellaire. Our father, bless his soul, had his share of shortcomings and one of them was stubbornness! When he got something in his mind, nobody could change it, come"hell or high-water." Well, Dad had the opinion that truck could carry about two times it's capacity load and therefore, he could shave two trips down to one, so on this trip, he failed the learning curve! They loaded and over-loaded and over-loaded to where the logs were piled several feet above the cab of the truck and the rear bed was almost setting on the back wheels. At that point they started home.

Stubborn as he was, Dad was an excellent driver and he knew he had to drive slowly to make it home without tipping the truck over. What he didn't figure in to his strategy, was the load capacity of the tires. The truck had dual rear wheels and they had two spares. However, that apparently didn't matter, as barely 10 miles later they had a flat tire and then another, and another. In all, they flattened 13 tires on that trip home and it took them 2 ½ days to get home!

The majority of that time was spent changing the tires and purchasing new ones. The funny thing was, they actually enjoyed the adventure of it, and bonded even further as father and son. They loved it, they were in "log-hauling hog-heaven" working hard with their hands and loving every minute of it. And, of course, it provided fodder for a great story and another lesson learned for both of them. "There are real reasons for <u>capacity ratings!</u>"

Another experience the bonding-boys shared was a short bicycle trip late one Saturday afternoon. Mother needed the family car for a shopping trip to Traverse City that would take her most of the day, so she dropped Dad off at work in the morning but had not yet returned when he needed a ride home. Dad called home and asked Bud to ride his bicycle out to the shop and pick him up. The total distance was about a mile and a half one-way and they would ride double on the way back with Bud on the handle- bars. <u>A great idea and a good time would be had by all</u>! Right? See what you think! Everything went smoothly at first. Bud picked up Dad and they were riding home, tooling down the highway with Bud on the handle-bars, up and down the hills, lots of fun! Well, did I mention that Dad was about 6' 3" and weighed 245 lbs.? An important factor that figures into this little escapade and Dad's stubbornness for capacity ratings. You remember me mentioning that Warner Bridge on the west side of town where it crosses the river? Well, just west of the bridge there is a big hill commonly known as Warner-Hill. Dad and Bud were having a great time as they came over the crest of the hill and headed down it as fast as Dad could pedal the thing toward the bridge. Dad hadn't had this much fun in years, pedaling frantically, wind blowing thru his hair, a big smile on his face and Bud's eyes as big as saucers, half laughing and half in fear!

Then, all of a sudden, <u>disaster struck</u>! About two-thirds of the way down the hill, doing about 30 miles per hour, <u>the front axle broke!</u> It snapped like a broken twig, and while the front wheel went on a personal tour of the west side of town, the front fork of the bicycle spread open as it slammed into the ground. It knifed into the loose gravel on the side of the road and Bud and Dad sailed gracefully into space a while, then tumbled <u>"ass-over-applecart"</u> down the embankment into the river in one big splash beside the bridge!

Now they both knew how to swim which wasn't really necessary, because it wasn't very deep and somehow, with the exception of a few bumps and scratches, neither was seriously hurt.

I was in the front yard when they came limping home, their clothes all wet and torn and carrying multiple pieces of bicycle. Somehow, they still managed to have broad grins on their faces when I asked them what had happened. They must have felt like fools walking through town like that, but I think they took the alley route to avoid having to walk on Main Street where all of the people could see them. Imagine the embarrassment! That would get them by the business district at least, but they would still have to walk two more blocks up the north hill to our house. Certainly a day to remember, bonding with Dad, and yet another lesson learned! I think dad was re-living his childhood when he did things like that with Bud. Most all equipment, even bicycles, have <u>capacity ratings!</u> What the hell, as the old saying goes, you live and learn and learning is what makes life worth living. Dad was a real character and while I didn't fully realize it at the time, I loved him a lot and as the years pass by, I miss him more each day.

Dad and Bud "Bonding"

Chapter Twenty: Hunting

I don't know what it is about the sport of hunting, and a lot of people wouldn't call it a sport. I liked it so much it was as if it was bred in me. I just felt it was something I had to do. No, I don't particularly cherish the thought of killing an animal or anything else, for that matter. To me it was more like a game between the animal and me. A game of wits to see who could outsmart the other. Of course, if I won, they would lose their life and if they won, they would live for another day, but there would be no ill consequence for me. It doesn't seem very fair in the scheme of things, does it? However, the other school of thought is that animals were put on earth to feed and nourish mankind. For thousands of years, this has been the way it was. Man would not have survived this long without animals as food and perhaps it was this instinct that fired my passion for it. I certainly did not hunt anything that was not edible. Even the ducks, as much as I personally disliked the meat, my parents did and I provided for them.

Usually I hunted by myself and occasionally, one of my friends would accompany me, depending upon the circumstance. With my parents owning quite a bit of land, I never ran out of places to hunt and didn't need an older person with me, as required by law for hunters under the age of 17. Because I was hunting on my own land, this was an exception under the law.

One early Saturday morning during deer season, I went hunting with two older high school friends, Bud Lewis and Bob Schoof. Bud was driving his dad's flat bed truck and the three of us were packed into the cab with our unloaded guns. We decided to try our luck in the hills a short way past the school on Orchard Hill Road. We drove up an old dirt trail towards a little abandoned hunting cabin that had been there for years. As we came around the last curve where the cabin was, "lo and behold" there were several deer standing directly in front of us next to the cabin. They had probably just come out of the old apple orchard a short ways behind the cabin, but there they were. We must have been down wind from them because they were not spooked at the sight of us piling out of the truck and trying to load our guns at the same time. They just stood there, about 50 ft away staring at us.

Have you ever heard of the term "buck fever?" Well if you haven't, here is the perfect example of it. Bud Lewis had a double barrel shot gun. It was the easiest gun to load so he was the first on the scene, so to speak. He jammed on the brakes, nearly throwing Bob and I through the windshield, and half fell out of his door as he tried to load his gun at the same time. Bud was a big guy, about 6'1" and 300 pounds. His feet had no sooner hit the ground than he began "lumbering" as fast as he could in the direction of the deer. He was so excited that he began to whoop and holler and pulling the triggers as fast as he could. "blam,! blam!," his gun bellowed as he ran! Then, just silence! Nothing happened! At this point, Bud was only 30 ft from the deer and they just stood there! Bud came to a screeching halt and also just stood there with his mouth and eyes wide open, his tongue hanging out, and an incredulous look on his face. He had missed all of them at point blank range! How could that be? At that moment, the deer got a whiff of us and took off in all directions as Bob and I began firing our guns. None of us managed to hit a damn thing, but at least Bob and I had the excuse that we were firing at moving targets. Bud, on the other hand, had just experienced a perfect case of good ole <u>buck fever!</u>" He would be the blunt of our jokes for many days to come. We said to him, "Did you have blanks in your gun?" Did you even take time to aim it?" "Why didn't you just throw the damn gun at them, you probably could have hit one of them that way."

Early one morning before daylight, I loaded up my 22-caliber Ranger semi-automatic rifle my uncle Merle had given me and headed out west of town to the apple orchard on my parents farm. As you all know by now, deer love to feed on apples and the countryside in northern Michigan is full of them. This orchard was a 40- acre tract of land on the north side of the highway just across the street from the cabin mill. I had checked it out the day before and there were a zillion deer tracks in the snow around the apple trees. This morning I crept quietly up the slope from the road to a spot where I could survey a good share of the orchard at first light. I was very good at being still and quiet and didn't move a muscle for about 30 minutes as I leaned against a tree. It was nearly light when suddenly I was aware of something to the left of my head. Very slowly I turned my head to the left and stared straight into the eyes of a deer about 6 inches off of my nose. In one swift moment, I raised my gun as the startled deer jumped and then stood sideways about 20 feet from me. It was buck season only and although I wasn't sure, I thought I saw short antlers in the limited light. I fired once and the deer ran off, as did the others I hadn't noticed standing nearby. When it was light enough, I walked in the direction the deer had run looking for blood in the snow but couldn't find any sign of it. I couldn't believe I had completely missed the deer because I was a pretty good shot but there was absolutely nothing to follow.

As I walked back to town, I told several people I met along the way about my strange encounter and about an hour later, there was a knock at my door. It was Les Miles, the game warden who just happened to live next door to us. Les was a friend of the family but he had a wary eye about "me and my hunting ethics." I guess he figured I would break the law somewhere along the way and neighbor or not, he would nail me for it!

News had spread quickly around town about the deer that had "licked my ears," while I had fallen asleep in an apple orchard and being half-asleep, I just started shooting at anything that moved. Now obviously, that is not the way I told the story, but in an hour's time in a small town, that's what it had developed into.

Les asked me where I had been hunting and did I hit the deer I shot at. I guess he wanted to make sure I hadn't shot a doe and just left it there to die. I told Les the truth about what had happened and said I tried to trail the deer but there was no blood trail to follow and there were so many tracks I soon lost the trail. I told him it was a young buck I had shot at but evidently had missed it completely.

My good reputation stayed intact that day because Les returned later and informed me that he could not find anything either. He was constantly lecturing me about not breaking the law as it was his duty to prosecute me if I did, even though we were neighbors. For some reason, Les was sure I would someday make a mistake due to my youth and the fact that I had usually hunted alone on my own property. Ha! I proved him wrong again!

There was another occasion the following fall when I had a close call with the game warden, although this time it wasn't Les Miles. My friend, Jack Matthew and I had decided to do a little duck hunting. Neither of us were 17 yet, and the law says you must be seventeen to hunt without an adult in the hunting party. Jack and I had taken my small boat down the Intermediate River south of town. We both had shotguns that were not loaded in case we happened to run into a game warden. As we drifted down the river we were fortunate (or not) not to see any ducks on the drift down to Lake Bellaire. Our plan was to drift down the river and then go west along the shoreline and work back into the "Lost channel" that ran behind the beach. This was a swampy marshland that usually hid an abundance of ducks and other wildlife. As we drifted down the river, and had the opportunity to see ducks, our plan was to quickly load our guns, shoot the ducks and then beach the boat on the west side of the river because my parents owned all of that land from Warner Bridge to Lake Bellaire and west of the river on the beach for a mile and a half on the north side of the lake. We would probably be breaking the law if we shot a duck on the river but if we weren't "caught in the act" by a warden, we would be safe on the shore- line of our property. So technically we could hunt from the shoreline or from the beach on the lake without adult supervision, or for that matter, even without a license. At least, I could. I didn't know about Jack, but if we were on private property, I don't think a warden would have jurisdiction there and Jack would be my guest anyway.

As we drifted down the river, we carried our shotgun shells in one hand and open-broached guns in the other. As it turned out, the only ducks we saw coming down the river were too far away and out of range for our guns. Shotguns with bird pellets were only good for a range of about 50 yards or so, and at that range the pellets would be so scattered, your chances of a hit were slim. That wouldn't necessarily be the case if the shells were loaded with buckshot. They would be fairly successful up to about 100 yards but you would really have to be a good shot to hit a flying duck at that range and if you did hit one, the buckshot would blow the bird to bits. Shotguns are considered fairly safe in a semi-populated hunting area because of the limited range. On the other hand, big game rifles have a range of several miles and therefore outlawed in populated areas. Rifles have only one projectile per shot so it calls for better accuracy on the part of the hunter. But, getting back to my story.

We paddled quietly west along the north shore of Lake Bellaire and into the hidden entrance of "The Lost Channel." We had loaded our shotguns in anticipation of getting a shot and were almost instantly rewarded. Just around the first bend, there was a "hellacious clatter" about 20 yards away as 4 beautiful Mallard ducks rose out of the water. If you have ever been duck hunting this way, you know when the ducks are surprised, they raise out of the water flapping their wings and quacking loudly, and it scares the hell out of you, even when you are expecting it. Jack and I both had single- shot guns and we both bagged a duck with our shots. There may have been more ducks in the lost channel that day but they were either frightened away by our commotion or another source that we soon discovered as we silently made our way to the other end of the channel. There, just around the last bend was another boat powered by the silent paddle strokes of a game warden! We were instantly surprised, to say the least, and we didn't know this man in the uniform of a game warden. This was Les Miles territory, but it certainly wasn't Les. He politely asked to see our licenses and noted that we had two dead ducks in the boat and certain proof of our hunt. Our goose was cooked, so to speak, if he had reason to nail us! He then asked us for our guns and stated that we were too young to be hunting without adult supervision and thus, were breaking the law. As we handed our guns over, I blurted out, "but this is our own property, we aren't hunting illegally." At this point he seemed sympathetic to our plight. He asked "are you sure this is your land?" I said "absolutely!" " It belongs to my family and clearly we are not breaking the law here." He gave us back our guns, apologized for not knowing the territory, and went on his way. After he was around the bend and out of sight, Jack and I grinned and let out a big sigh of relief. Both of our parents were prominent businessmen in town and our arrest surely would have created a big scandal.

Later, when Les Miles returned to town, he came to see me and told me he had heard about the incident from the other warden. He said we were lucky because he would have arrested us due to the fact we were in a boat on the water and therefore not on private property. In retrospect, I'm not so sure Les was right about that. The "Lost Channel" was not a chartered waterway and whether or not it was part of our property would have to be determined by an expensive survey of the lake frontage. Something neither party would have been eager to undertake and due to the fact that you are innocent until proven guilty, I think the burden would have fallen on the Department of Conservation. All in all, I think this was just another attempt on Les's part to intimidate me. I was not really a "loose cannon" as he thought. I just loved to hunt and fish like my forefathers did and if it appeared that I bent the rules a little bit, it was just because of my enthusiasm for the sport and not from any malicious intent.

Chapter Twenty One: Basketball

Prior to moving to Bellaire, my athletic abilities were quite limited. I was still growing and a bit clumsy due to that rapid growth. I didn't reach that peak of growth until the age of 15 or 16. I could throw a stone a long way and run pretty fast, but that was about it. I had been introduced to basketball in 7th grade before moving up to Bellaire but it was a very limited experience. Then in Bellaire as I entered the 8th grade, it was a different ball game, so to speak. Everybody played basketball, and because of my height and jumping prowess, I became one of the elite and sought after on weekend pick-up games.

We had a junior-high team that played 4 or 5 other schools and were coached by our new school superintendent, Bill Boerner. Bill loved the game but I don't believe he ever played because of his diminutive stature. He was only about 5'5" tall and now beginning to age with a pretty good paunch in front, balding with gray side-burns and wore glasses. He idolized the university of Kentucky basketball team and their coach who preferred the fast-break method of transition scoring. Bill, was a genuinely nice guy, a good coach and we all loved him. I say "<u>we</u>" meaning his players but not necessarily our parents. Some of them thought he spent too much of his time coaching and not enough on his duties as superintendent of schools. As far as I knew, my parents were not among the nay-sayers but he certainly had a number of other critics.

He coached us well and we didn't lose a game that year. I made the varsity squad as a freshman the next year as we again went undefeated until the regional tournaments. In my sophomore year, we repeated as a powerhouse, especially with the new addition of a tall center. Six foot six, Johnny Overpool had just moved to the area but knew nothing about the game. Coach Boerner had moved up as varsity coach and made it his personal project to turn Johnny into a star. John was tall and thin with long arms and all he had to do was stand there and hold the ball high over his head and nobody could reach it. He couldn't jump very high, but he didn't have to and he could gather in anything that came within 15 feet of him. He would then pass it off to one of our scorers on a drive to the basket and we were unstoppable. We won game after game and had the highest per game scoring average of any team north of Grand Rapids according to the Grand Rapids Press. They also rated us as one of the top Class D teams in the state.

Come tournament time that year one Saturday morning and the day of a big game, Coach Boerner thought he would take Lyle Jensen and I on a trip to Traverse City with him and his family to get our minds off of the game for a few hours, hence we wouldn't be so nervous at game time. Actually, he was the nervous one, not Lyle and I, but we went along to appease him. Coach had an old 37 Chevrolet sedan and he put his wife and 12 year old daughter in the front seat with him while Lyle and I shared the back seat. But, before I finish this little story, I have to give you a little more background about our remarkable coach <u>Boerner</u>!

Next to his family, the thing that Bill loved the most was coaching his team. He had a bunch of good athletes here and he thought he could take us all to the state Class D championship. Lyle, Bill Crandall and I were the top scorers on the team and the Ski Valley Conference as well. Every year we played, Lyle and I were the top 2 scorers in the Conference and Bill was a close 3rd.

During a game, coach Boerner was a nervous wreck. He was so bad, he couldn't watch the play! He would sit on the bench with his head hung down chewing on his tie like it was an enormous piece of pizza! He would chew it, spit it out and ask the player sitting next to him what was happening on the floor! They would answer and then he would commence chewing on his tie again until there was another roar from the crowd, whereby his ritual would begin all over again.

When the game was over and we had won, he would spit out his dripping wet, ghastly looking tie, pop on his hat and coat and walk home leaving his family and car parked somewhere downtown, completely oblivious to anything except savoring his team's win. He, of course, had forgotten his family and his car! It didn't matter anyway, because if he did remember his car, he had absolutely no recollection where he parked it, so he couldn't find it anyway. The next day he would then walk back downtown, locate his car and drive it home. His wife and daughter finally wised up to him and stayed home. They had gotten tired and embarrassed of hitching rides from friends after the game and trying to explain why Bill didn't drive them home. He was eccentric, but we loved him anyway. Now back to my story. This Saturday morning, as we putted along the highway to Traverse City at the alarming speed of 35 miles per hour, Bill had taken a short cut down the then, dirt road past Williamsburg. The road was straight but with short hills like moguls on a ski run and Coach was deep in thought! He didn't have a real good view due to his short stature and he could barely see over the steering wheel most of the time. Add to that the fact that he had his left elbow propped against the door and his broad-brimmed hat tipped slightly forward nearly covering his eyes. From the back seat, he was quite a sight and Lyle and I couldn't help chuckling to ourselves as we watched him sit there like he was in a trance.

There was very little traffic on the road that day and you could see a long ways ahead even over the hills. No cars were coming from the other direction but there was one in front of us that Bill decided to pass. We were going bout 35mph and I guess the other car was traveling about 34 or 34 ½ mph and you knew this was going to take a while. So we began passing him and passing him, and passing him, up the hill, down the hill, up the hill, down the hill! After about five minutes or so, it became apparent to everyone except Bill who was in another world somewhere, that this little maneuver wasn't going to happen this day or maybe for a week!

Bill's wife began to give him little, quick concerned glances of which he paid absolutely no attention to whatsoever. He was obviously deep in thought or perhaps half asleep. Just then, the driver of the other car also became nervous and swerved slightly whereby Bill's wife shouted <u>"BILL!" and abruptly woke him from his stupor!</u> It startled him so that his arms began to flail at the wheel, his hat fell down over his eyes and all Lyle and I could see from the back seat was the top of his bald head as he kept flailing his arms at the steering wheel. The car went off the road on the left side part way up an embankment and rolled over on it's top as it slid back onto the surface of the road and came to a stop!

In the back seat, I was on the bottom inside the roof. The back seat was on top of me and Lyle on the top of the seat. Bill's wife and child were OK but as she called out Bill's name he didn't answer. Frantically, she called again and this time he finally answered, "I'm OK, what happened?" We opened the doors and crawled out only to discover that the other driver had fled the scene completely, probably not wanting to get involved. Not one of us had gotten a scratch and Lyle and I began to smile and chuckle a little from the relief of stress I guess. Bill noticed that one of the front wheels had turned inward from a broken steering arm. He instinctively grabbed it and tried to straighten the wheel. Instantly, his feet slipped out from under him and he fell flat on his ass! <u>That did it!</u> Lyle and I could no longer hold it in and we bellowed out with laughter at the pathetic sight of Bill laying on his ass and the memory of the whole experience that led up to it! Coaches' wife looked at us with a horrified expression and then also began to smile. I guess the unusual experience was at first traumatic to her, but then she realized that no one was hurt and the whole scene, although pitiful, was also, pathetically hilarious!

Just then, another car pulled up. It was the Semrau's from Bellaire, also on their way to Traverse City, for a day of shopping. The Semrau girls bounded out of their car and offered comfort to Lyle and I if we needed it! We didn't, of course, but it was nice to have them fawning over us just the same. Coach walked to the nearest farmhouse and called a tow truck. Then we all piled into Semrau's car and drove on into Traverse City. Later that afternoon, when we returned to

Bellaire, the whole town had already heard about the accident and many people, including all of the team cheerleaders, were waiting for us on main-street. Again we were fawned over with many hugs and kisses. Everyone was happy that their' basketball stars had not been injured in the accident! I tell you, it was well worth doing it all over again.

Coach did accomplish one thing. He took our minds off of the big game. By game time, we were completely relaxed and went on to an easy victory. Coach was a "hoot!"

Coach Boerner fulfilling his promise

Chapter Twenty Two: Bill Crandall

Even though Lyle Jensen was my closest friend, I also spent a lot of time with Bill Crandall. Bill owned an old Model A Ford coupe and late one summer he asked me to accompany him on a trip to the Northwestern Michigan Fair at Traverse City. Our plan was to drive to Traverse, spend the night in his car and come back home the next day. Sleeping in his car wasn't going to be very comfortable but we didn't care, we couldn't afford a hotel room and it would be a good adventure for us!

Everything went smoothly until we arrived in Traverse City. Just before we got to the fairground, we heard a siren and a local cop pulled us over. What ticked us both off is that was absolutely no reason for that cop to stop us! We weren't speeding, Heaven knows that old car couldn't go over 45 mph if it had to. We had not gone through a red light, a stop sign or otherwise broken the law. That cop just saw an old car with out of town license and two young guys in it and just presumed we were guilty of something. As he checked Bill's license, we both asked him repeatedly why he stopped us but our questions were just ignored. Finally he said, "shut up and get out of the car or I will take you both to jail!" That did the trick. He was a bully and we did just as we were told. He proceeded to check everything on the car from end to end trying to find something wrong with it. Then as a last resort, he got in the car and pushed hard on the brake pedal. "Aha" he said gleefully, "your brakes are bad!" " I'm going to impound this vehicle until you get them repaired!" This was ridiculous! We all knew, including the stupid cop that there was nothing wrong with the brakes. Yes, they were old mechanical brakes that were standard on the old cars and not hydraulic ones, but they worked fine at normal speed and they couldn't be improved upon except for small adjustments. This cop just wanted to be a bad-ass, and he was!

Well, we went to the fair, on-foot. We spent the small amount of money we each had and along the way, added to our sexual education a bit. There was one particular freak show that got our attention. There were the usual, strange, malformed personalities that end up in freak shows and at the end of the show, the barker said, **"ladies and gentlemen, for those of you who wish to stay and pay**

**an additional 2 dollars, we will show you Ginger, who
is half man and half woman!"** Bill and I looked at each
other and quickly dug into our pockets for an additional 2
dollars. Shortly, a butt-ugly woman appeared dressed in a
full- length robe. She promptly disrobed and stood there
naked. A skinny old man standing beside us began to laugh
loudly at the sight. I guess he hadn't seen a naked woman in
some time and this was his way of expressing his pleasure,
or displeasure. At the barker's directions, the gal spread
her legs slightly and said, "you see, she has both a female
vagina and a man's penis!" Whereby the gal reached down
and palmed a short piece of loose flesh next to her vagina.
"And it doesn't interfere with intercourse either," as she
began to masturbate in front of us. The old man laughed
louder! Needless to say, Bill and I just stared in disbelief and
shock! Neither of us had ever seen anything as bizarre as this
before! As we walked away bewildered, we agreed, the only
thing to do was to chalk it up to our continuing education
of lifetime experiences.

We had no car for the long trip home or to sleep in
either. We had planned to spend the night so now we had
a huge problem. There was a lakeside park across the street
from the fairgrounds and we thought we could probably
sleep on a couple of the benches. As darkness fell we gave it
a try. What a night! There was no way to get comfortable
on those darn things. I tossed and turned and when I finally

started to slumber, <u>I was abruptly awakened by Bill shaking</u> <u>me and saying, come on, we have to get out of here, run!</u>" I struggled to my feet and followed him down the road about a hundred yards where he jogged to a stop and I asked, "what happened?" "What's the matter?" He said, "I was half asleep and had to pee. I thought I was peeing on an old log in the bushes and then realized I was pissing on a drunken Indian laying on the ground in the dark!" "The guy swore at me, got up and began chasing me a ways, but I think we have lost him now." Like I said, "what a night!"

Later, after daylight, we walked up the street to a restaurant, got some breakfast and went back to the fair. After all, that was our plan and we were sticking to it! A couple of hours later, we found where they had taken Bill's car and tried to get it back. Unfortunately, for us, they would not release it, which left us with yet another dilemma. How the hell were we going to get back home? We were left with no choice but to "hitch-hike." Back then," hitch-hiking" was not dangerous and I resorted to it many times again. Once was with my girl friend Nancy. We "hitch-hiked" all the way from East Lansing to Detroit, a distance of about 60 miles. " Hitch-hiking" was quite common after the 2nd world war because they stopped building cars during the war and a lot of people had no other way of transportation. You wouldn't dare think of doing it anymore. There are too many "kooks" on the roads nowadays.

It took us several hours to finally get back to Bellaire. It was only 35 miles, but it seemed to take forever. I went to bed at 4:30 that afternoon and slept until 10 AM the next morning. So much for that little adventure!

Chapter Twenty Three: SOLO'S

There was a time in the school year of 48 or 49 that an Athletic Awards Banquet was being held in the basement of Bellaire Community Hall. A special guest, former Detroit Tiger baseball player and then sports announcer for the Tigers, "Harry Hielman" was to be in attendance.

Some poor misinformed soul had been told that Bill Crandall and Bill Lovett, prominent members of the Bellaire sports teams were also good musicians in the band and requested our appearances for "solos" as entertainment for the banquet. It was entertainment all right, but not the kind it was intended to be!

I can't remember who the culprit was, but I am thinking it was Jack Matthews and Jack, I apologize if it wasn't you, but you were always playing pranks on us in retribution for our shameful treatment of you. So I'm thinking it was you!

Anyway, Bill and I were told that eating "saltine crackers" just prior to our performance would quiet our nerves and enhance our abilities! (Are you getting the picture here?) Poor Bill C. was first up with a trombone solo accompanied by pianist Joyce Dunson. Thank Heaven Joyce didn't have to eat saltine crackers to solidify her performance. Hers was flawless!

So Joyce played the intro and Crandall started his performance, -- and started! - - and started!--, but no matter how hard he blew on that damn horn, nothing came out but air! Pfffffffffffft,---pffffffffffft,----pfffffffffffft! Nothing! Poor Bill, everyone in town knew that when he got frustrated or embarrassed, <u>HE GOT RED!!!! His cheeks bulged and the harder he tried, the redder he got!</u> Joyce glanced at him nervously, stopped and restarted the intro, and still, <u>NOTHING!</u>

<u>Finally, on the third restart, there was a very loud –</u> "<u>BLAAAAHH!</u> Bill experienced a <u>"profound breakthrough"</u>! Through his frustration, he finally had succeeded in developing enough saliva to get a noise out of the instrument and went on to complete his solo.

Now it was my turn on the Cornet and I was scared stiff! Was the same thing going to happen to me? Everybody in the audience were all smiles and I was white as a sheet! I had eaten some crackers too, but luckily, being the second to perform, had some time to conjure up a bit of saliva in my dry mouth to give me a decent chance at success. As it turned out, I was only a few notes short and Joyce was able to adjust quickly enough to provide an excellent job of accompaniment. Whew! What a relief it was when that was over!

The next day, our entire baseball team was invited to have a private interview with Mr. Hielman at Edith Richard's home on Cayuga Street. In the course of conversation, Harry asked, "who, among you here is going to be a baseball star?" They all pointed to me and he said, "I hope you are a better ball player than you are a horn blower! Embarrassing!

Chapter Twenty Four: Team Trip

After the baseball season during my junior year in high school, coach George Brown talked the school into providing funds to take our victorious team to Detroit to see the Tigers play. The school bought our tickets and provided a school bus for the trip, but we had to pay our own meal expenses. It was just a one- day trip, so we left early in the morning and returned that same night after the game. It was a pretty cushy trip for everyone except the bus driver. Down and back was a drive of over 500 miles and about 12 hours on the road. I don't remember his name, but he was a good sport and didn't complain. After all, he got to see the game too.

The game was great, the Tigers won, we all had a good time and the trip was fairly uneventful. I say "fairly" because the return trip did have a couple of hitches. One of our outfielders was Delbert Crandall, a cousin of Bill Crandall. We all called him "goofy" because he reminded us of the

Disney character "Goofy the Dog." Goof was a good kid, easy going, long and lanky, not very coordinated and had a hilarious laugh. It was really the laugh that gave him his nickname.

The long ride home was tedious and boring and a number of the guys were sleeping in their seats, including Delbert. He had his head back with his mouth wide open and snoring loudly when one of the guys got an idea. Someone had been peeling an orange and the peelings were just lying there waiting to be utilized by some enterprising sneaky villain. As we all watched gleefully, one of the guys (not me) popped a big piece of orange peel into Delbert's "wide open mouth." He sucked it in then coughed, choked, coughed some more and then spit it out big time along with some other "flim-flam" he had eaten some time before. It was great fun and laughter for everyone except Goofy and of course, those who were sitting directly in front of him! He opened his eyes big as saucers and lurched forward as he "hurled" over a number of his laughing spectators. True to form, after his coughing spree, he realized he was again the brunt of someone's joke and laughed along with the rest of us. In retrospect, it was a stupid trick because he could have literally choked to death! Kids don't think of the consequences of their actions sometimes until it's too late. Wouldn't that have put a damper on the fun trip!

As we neared home, about 30 miles out, someone asked, "where's Eugene?" Eugene Kent was the youngest kid in the group. He was only a freshman, and until this trip, had never been outside of Antrim County. He wasn't on the bus and because he was such a quiet kid, no one had missed him until then. Coach was frantic! It was his responsibility and he had failed to count everyone before we left the stadium. We stopped the bus at the next town and coach called the Detroit police to try to locate him. Luckily, Eugene had more sense than we gave him credit for. He had called home and arrangements were made to bring him back to Bellaire on a Greyhound bus. Coach Brown was quite embarrassed by the whole ordeal but it worked out OK. I think he had to pay for the bus ticket and he was happy to get off that easily!

Chapter Twenty Five:
Bellaire Golf Club

During the second full summer after our move to Bellaire, my parents implored upon me to get a job. What a revolting idea! I guess just providing fish and game for the family table didn't take up enough of my idle time and they wanted to make sure it was spent in a positive manner. In other words, they wanted to keep me out of the pool hall and out of trouble, especially since the canoe incident the previous summer. Lyle and I put our heads together and decided we would caddy at the Bellaire Golf Club. It wasn't bad work except when we were asked to carry double (two bags apiece) and it gave us a little money for snacks and a few games of pool at the local pool parlor. We all liked the couple who owned the pool parlor. They were good people and very nice to all of the school kids who frequented the place.

At that time, the Golf Club was owned and operated by Paul Krager and his wife, Madeline. Neither of them were golf professionals but they did know the basics of the game that they could teach to absolute beginners and if anyone wanted a professional lesson, they would turn them over to Del Lynn, Bill Crandall's stepfather. Del was also the greens-keeper at the course and although he wasn't a card carrying pro, he was a damn good golfer and held the course record there of 32 on the par 37 nine hole course. Del was a genuinely nice guy and very good with people. He told me he thought it was possible, if someone played a perfect game, to score a 29 on the course, but he had not been able to break 32 yet. Ironically, years later at age 43, I would break Del's record with a 31. That record still held until they changed the course to 18 holes a few years ago. That being the case, my record of 31 on the original nine-hole course will stand forever. That's my legacy I guess, and the only "Claim to Fame" I'll ever have.

Being a caddy wasn't all that exciting. We would get a set once a day or so and for $1.50 per round or $3.00 for double bags, we certainly weren't getting rich. Most of our spare time was spent looking for lost balls in the woods. The ones we found were sold by Paul in the clubhouse as "experienced" balls for about 1/3rd the cost of new ones so we made a little extra on the side. The caddies went out in rotation so no one had an advantage and with 4 or 5 caddies vying for a set each day, we had a little friendly competition.

Jim and Dick Alspaugh were two of the other caddies. They lived about a block away from me on the north side of town and we were quite often able to share a ride to the course. One day a foursome of wealthy, elderly, pot-bellied cottage owners came to play and they all wanted caddies so Lyle and I and the Alspaugh brothers got the jobs at the same time. The old duffers were all dressed up in knickers, knee-high argyle socks, colorful vests and riding caps and they certainly looked the part of vogue golfers. Jim and Dick were fun guys and Dick especially was a real "cut-up"! He was great for "one-liners" and I knew we were going to be in trouble on the very first tee. As I said, the golfers were elderly and not very coordinated. When the first one on the tee whiffed his first swing, Dick began to chuckle. The rest of us turned away so the players wouldn't see the smiles on our faces, but Dick stood right in there, cackling like a chicken! We tried to shut him up. After all $1.50 was $1.50 and big money at the moment! The guy finally managed to hit the ball in the right direction between dirty glances to Dick for his disrespect, and we all gained our composure – for- awhile ! Our half-hidden smiles and silent chuckles continued as the old guys had their troubles making contact with the ball. They were getting extremely frustrated as the game wore on and our little antics did nothing to help the situation. By now they were all giving us dirty looks and a bit of chastising as well. I guess they figured they were paying us big money of $1.50 for lugging their heavy bags and locating lost balls during our two-hour leisurely stroll and we should be more respectful for being paid so well!

Dick began talking to his employer a bit and tried to give him some good-natured advice about his swing. As we approached the 3rd tee, the man asked him what the yardage was for the hole. Dick replied "389 yards" and the old geezer quipped, "just a hell of a drive and a putt, right?" Everybody chuckled good-naturedly at the comment as the sorry fellow waggled to the tee. On this hole, a small creek runs across the fairway about 20 yard in front of the tee box and flows into the Trout pond back on the 2nd hole. The old boy teed up his ball, gazed down the fairway and with a big grunt, took a tremendous swing at the ball and nearly fell down! His club-head barely tipped the top of the ball and it trickled down the fairway 20 yards and into the creek. Dick couldn't contain himself any longer. "And now for a hell of a putt!" he blurted out and we all roared with laughter!

Unfortunately, for us, the old boys didn't quite see the humor in the situation and we were all fired on the spot! As we walked back to the clubhouse still laughing, Paul saw us coming and asked us what happened. Upon hearing the story, he chewed us out for failing in our duties as helpful caddies, then sat down and laughed with us as we relived the hilarious moment and Dick's "right-on" comment. Paul's wife Madeline, the stern one in the group, wasn't as understanding and threatened our jobs if we ever did anything like that again.

Sometime that summer, the Kragers sold the golf club to a couple named Lil and Don Sitch. Don was a golf-professional and Lil had been a featured vocalist with one of the famous touring Big Bands at the time. They were great people and Don was a super salesman that could sell a refrigerator to an Eskimo. Both were community oriented and donated a lot of their time to various town projects.

When the Kragers moved away, they left their dog, "Buster", with the golf course. He loved it there at the course, and it would have been cruel to take him away. Buster was something else, a mid sized, black and white, mixed breed Border- Collie and the smartest animal I have ever seen!

There was an old war surplus jeep in the tractor shed that was the main piece of equipment on the course. Don used it to mow the fairways, pull tree stumps and just plain old transportation when he drove the three miles into town. All of this time, Buster would ride on the hood of the jeep whether it was looking for ground squirrels while mowing fairways or the trip into town. The ground squirrels would burrow holes in the fairways and it was Buster's job to eliminate them and he did a damn good job of it. He would ride the jeep until he spotted one and then jump off and run the critters down before they could get to their burrow hole. Buster earned his keep! We would take him to the Trout pond or Creek where he would walk the bank until he saw a Trout and then dive into the ice-cold water, swim underwater and grab the fish in his mouth and proudly present it to us. He wasn't successful every time, but his percentages were high. I've never seen any animal do that before or since!

When Don drove into town, he usually took the open jeep and Buster would ride on the hood the whole trip. Thirty five to fifty miles per hour facing the wind never fazed him. He looked like an oversized hood ornament! Strangers on the road were amazed and aghast at the sight and Buster became a local celebrity evoking many news stories and pictures in local newspapers. That was not the end of Buster's accomplishments. He could also climb trees! Yes, you heard me right, "climb trees!" Don nailed an old sock about ten feet up on a two-foot diameter Elm tree by the clubhouse and upon his command, Buster would shimmy up that tree with all four legs and grab that sock. He would hang there shaking the sock from side to side until it came off the tree, then shimmy back down the tree and present Don with his prize.

Don delighted in showing off Buster's skills to people and especially young kids. He would tell them that Buster was a multilingual dog and understood French as well as English. To prove it he would say, "Chevrolet Coupe, Buster"! Buster would pick up his ears and bark once. Of course, the kids wouldn't realize that when Don said Buster's name at the end, he simply reacted to hearing his name. Don could do the same with a phrase in any language and get the same results.

One summer day when Lyle and I showed up at the course for our caddie work, we were surprised to see a bunch of brand-new pull carts next to the caddie shack. Don came out and announced that from then on he was giving the golfers an alternative method of carrying their bags. Only this method would make him money and not us. We realized our days were numbered and it didn't take long for the end to come! We didn't get much work and we spent more time in the woods looking for balls that we could clean up and re-sell. Sure enough, we returned to the clubhouse one day with our cache of balls and Don confronted us. He angrily demanded "where were you guys? I had two players here looking for caddies and you weren't around! If you want to continue to work here you have to stay close to the clubhouse in case I need you. Do you want to work, or not?" Now with all due respect for Don, that was the wrong thing to say to us at that time! First he took away 75% of our rounds by purchasing golf carts and now he would prohibit us from making part of our deficit back by selling golf balls on the side? Lyle looked at me and I looked at him and we both said, <u>"to hell with it, let's go swimming</u>! We walked away and left Don standing there with his mouth agape and feeling very stupid. He didn't expect us to call his bluff. A week later he saw us in town and asked us to come back saying all was forgiven. We said "no, no more" and that was the end of our caddie-shack days and the end of caddies at the Bellaire Golf Club. We went on to do more important things, like selling t-shirts and rotten apples! After all, we were becoming' entrepreneurs!"

Chapter Twenty Six:
Before Nancy – Bill's Love Life

Early in my junior year of high school, Nancy Anger became my steady girlfriend. Before that, I had dated several girls and pretty much played the field. Primarily due to my athletic prowess as a "jock", I pretty much had my pick of the gals and I was quite choosy. "spoiled" would probably be a better word there. A couple of them kept me at bay. Eloise Bachelder and Marylyn Wilks. They were both beautiful girls, and good friends, but neither one would date me. For some reason, Eloise preferred boys who were from out of town and wouldn't give the locals a tumble. She dated "Shortie Shell" from Mancelona for a long time and they had a stormy off and on again relationship before their eventual break-up and she ended up marrying a good friend of mine, Bob Klooster from Ellsworth. Marylyn, on the other hand, dated an older man, Scotty Maltby, from Bellaire, for quite some time and ended up marrying him. Marylyn was a tall slender girl with long dark hair and a cheerleader for our basketball squad. She had a perpetual, teasing smile that captivated me, but there was never a chance for anything more. Eloise was also one of our cheerleaders. She was the gorgeous blond in the bunch and the team was very proud of all of them. They represented us, and the school, very well. I haven't seen either of the girls in years although I would run into Eloise in Charlevoix on occasion in the seventy's after I moved back to Bellaire with my family. She and Bob had a great family and lived close to his extended family in Atwood.

Another girl I dated a lot was Irma Klingelhofer. She lived north of town on a farm with her parents and two sisters. Irma was pretty, tall and lanky and a lot of fun. Her German parents were gracious, friendly people who threw many fun, clean parties for us teenagers and we loved to go there. Irma had a big crush on me at the time, which is probably why I never took her seriously and I liked her just as a good friend.

One cold winter weekend, Lyle's girlfriend, Gay, was staying in town with family friends and she invited Lyle, Irma and I over for the evening to play Pinochle. We were all well behaved kids who didn't drink, smoke or take drugs and spent a lot of time together playing cards, so it was going to be a nice pleasant evening enjoying each other's company.

The older couple Gay was staying with had gone out for the evening and left the house for the younger folks to enjoy. About 11:00 we had gotten tired of cards and got down to do some serious "smooching" on the couches in the living room. It then became easier to lie down on the couches and then the inevitable happened! <u>We all fell asleep!</u> (fooled you didn't I?) I told you we were good kids and we were. We just fell asleep! I don't remember the exact time when the s---. hit the fan. It was somewhere in the wee hours of the morning when we were suddenly and rudely awakened by a loud female voice exclaiming, "<u>well I never!</u>" We abruptly sat up and stared into the astonishing eyes of the old folks who had just returned home and thought they had caught us all in the act of having sex. Obviously, we all were still fully dressed and that should have been a clue that just maybe we had simply fallen asleep. Nevertheless, we were embarrassed and after many fruitless explanations and excuses, Lyle and I were sent packing and were quite fortunate that our parents weren't called! That would have really gotten us into trouble. Strange, but for some reason we were never invited over there again! Gay and Lyle ended up getting married after high school and have spent the rest of their lives together. Irma married my good friend and baseball catcher, Ordie Hierlihy and to the best of my knowledge they are still living happily in the Bellaire area.

I liked the kind of girls that were hard to get and I enjoyed the "chase". June Griffith was one of those. She was a sweet girl, good looking and had a great body. We dated several times but she would never even let me get to "first base" so I eventually lost interest in her. After high school, she married a nice local boy and moved to Lansing. Unfortunately, June succumbed to cancer at a very young age. That was tragic. She and her husband never had the chance to accumulate much in earthly possessions and to die without realizing the fulfillment of life," has no meaning!"

Then there was Susan, the "Trout Queen" from Mancelona. Every spring, the town of Kalkaska has a National Trout Festival and as one of the activities, they crown one of the local beauties. Susan was a gorgeous gal and had taken that crown the previous year. One of my high school buddies had dated her and bragged about his sexual conquest with the beauty. That intrigued me so, naturally, I looked up her phone number and asked her for a date. We had not met but she knew who I was from stories in the newspapers about my athletic accomplishments. She accepted my invitation and we took in a movie at the local theatre. After the show, I drove out to a lonely spot, parked and we proceeded to get "heated up". At that point in time, the local jargon for "petting" was "<u>smooching</u>" and a whole lot of that was going on! She pretty much let me have my way until I tried to get into her panties. She didn't say "no" but she grabbed my hand and pushed it away again and again but all the time kept me in a passionate lip-lock. Because she didn't complain, I kept trying harder and harder and she fought back harder and harder. Finally, I relented, apologized and said, "I'm sorry, I hope you don't hate me". I was completely surprised when she answered, "Oh No, not at all"! Obviously, she liked it, and I was reinvigorated. So with my superior strength, I succeeded in getting my hand inside her panties and found the magic touch. This time, instead of pushing my hand away, she used it to her own advantage and fulfillment. When she was finally satisfied, I said, "OK, now it is my turn" and tried to have sex with her. Unfortunately, for me, her desire had waned and she turned me down flatly with the statement, "we have no right to do that because we are not married!" I was stumped and needless to say, very frustrated! Now I understand how women get raped! But as smooth as I thought I was, I didn't have an answer for that one and I wasn't the forceful type, so I went home to a cold shower and dreams of another day. I don't know what she had in mind, but I certainly wasn't going to propose to her just to "get a little". As beautiful and curvaceous as she was, I didn't even know her before that evening and my parents didn't raise a stupid "Billy Boy". Horny as I was, my brain overtook my hormones and I backed off. I wasn't ready for matrimony, besides, there were hundreds and hundreds of girls out there and I was just beginning to sew my wild oats.

There were a lot of girls I had met that were "easy", but they didn't interest me. I was a passionate lover and thoroughly enjoyed the art of seduction. I loved the thrill of the chase and the girl had to be pretty, sexy, hard to get and SPECIAL!

Nancy was my true love and because she was and I had great respect for her, I never pressured her to consummate our relationship. Her parents were great people. I loved them and they loved me, so I would do nothing to disappoint them or embarrass my parents. Nancy and I were both willing to wait until our wedding night, which, as fate would have it, wasn't ever to be!

After high school graduation, I left Bellaire to attend college at Michigan State University and because of the distance between us, our romance slowly withered away. Nancy and I agreed that due to the situation, we would be free to date others but would leave the weekends open for each other when I could make the trip back to Bellaire. At the time, we didn't realize this arrangement would eventually lead to our split. It just so happened that after my graduation, my parents moved back to the Detroit area and Nancy's parents bought our house in Bellaire. They welcomed me to stay with them anytime I came home, so it appeared to be the perfect solution. I would come back about once a month and we would spend time together. It wasn't long before I noticed Nancy becoming resentful of my being there and her folks dictating that she had to spend time with me. She began dating other guys more frequently and enjoying those experiences. Being a vivacious and attractive girl with raging hormones that I wasn't satisfying just took it's toll on our relationship. Looking back, I should have been more aggressive with her and our lives might have been completely different. I have no doubt we would have been extremely happy together.

The summer after my freshman year at Michigan State, I was invited to come to Alden for the summer and play baseball for the Alden semi-pro team. I would live with Loyd Amisegger, the team owner-manager in his beautiful house on Torch Lake. Loyd gave me free room and board and $50. per week spending money. We kept our deal secret as I was still considered an amateur at Michigan State in order to stay eligible for their baseball program. It was a sweet deal for both of us as I had plenty of time to play around, didn't have to work and could court the ladies in my little red 1936 Ford roadster. I purchased this car the previous year as a skeleton. In other words, it consisted only of a body, engine, frame and wheels. I would search for several months at junk-yards around the state to find parts for this machine until I had finally gathered fenders, bumpers headlights and continental rear wheel for it. Then I rehabbed the entire car with a new top, upholstery, white sidewall tires and a shiny bright red paint job. Boy, what a beauty she was now and I was the envy of all my peers!

On Loyds behalf, he ran the ball club in Alden as a business, charging admission and also made profits from the concession stand. We drew a lot of fans due to the variety of teams scheduled from around the state and my notoriety as a local pitching phenomenon taking on all comers. We played 2 games a week and we won them all. I rarely gave up more than two or three hits and even pitched one more no-hitter to bring my career total to four by the age of 18. All of our games were played under the lights at night and many of the fans drove a long ways to see one of our games. One game on our schedule was a professional black team from Grand Rapids, the "Grand Rapids Black Sox". We drew a large crowd to see that game and we didn't disappoint them, winning quite handily. As good as they were, they couldn't solve the mystery of my "drop-off-the-table" curve, mixed with my fastball and change-up pitches. (It sure is fun to live in the past! Please forgive my shameful bragadosio. I just hope I haven't embellished this story too much to lose my credibility with you)!

That summer in Alden is where I met Helen. Ah yes, Helen! Loyd owned a small bait shop in town and I spent a couple of hours a day waiting on customers behind the counter. One day this cute little blond with a terrific body walked in and said "<u>hello</u>"! It was one of those moments that defy explanation, except to say, that we were immediately attracted to each other. I was so taken with her looks I almost fell out of my chair! Love at first sight? I don't know about that, but physically attracted, yes! After a little chit-chat, I learned she and her family were from Ohio and were renting a cottage by Clam River for a couple of weeks. We were both a little shy and awkward at the time and after a few minutes she left to join her parents. However, the next day she was back again, so I gathered my composure and asked her for a date. She smiled coyly and said "yes," I would love to go out with you", and that was the beginning of a 10 day, steamy hot romance! We went to the movies in Bellaire that night and parked in the woods for a little "smooching" afterwards but she wouldn't let me get to 2nd base. She politely rebuffed my foreign advances (Russian hands and Roman fingers).

We went out again the next night and "boy" were things different the 2nd time around! I had no sooner picked her up when she giggled and remarked, "I just remembered I have my shorts on under my skirt"! I looked at her a little puzzled and then realized she expected me to discover that little bit of information for myself, later on in the evening. I had anticipated some action that night and had borrowed Loyd's wife's car because it had a back seat that my little red car did not have and didn't lend itself to lovemaking for the only position I was aware of with my little experience. We decided to skip the show and go directly to the woods! We were both hot as firecrackers and the smooching quickly turned to serious business! We tore off our clothes and clambered into the back seat when all of a sudden, I discovered I had a big problem. I was 6'4" and that back seat was only 5' long. I finally realized I could put my feet out of the window but it was still a bit uncomfortable because the back window wouldn't go all the way down and the glass hurt my shins. After a little adjusting I said "to hell with it", for what I was about to get, it was worth skinning up my shins a little and it certainly was! I was having the time of my life and she was fantastically insatiable!

On the short ride home, I began to smell something fishy, I MEAN " REALLY FISHY", and I mentioned it to Helen. I said, "do you smell stinky fish? What a terrible smell!" I was driving Martha's car so I presumed she had gone to the fish market that day and forgotten to take it out of the trunk. I was obviously very naïve about these things and honestly didn't realize how I had embarrassed Helen until I asked Martha the next day if she had left fish in the trunk of the car? Martha and Loyd rolled with laughter for ten minutes before they could compose themselves enough to explain to me what the odor was. Man, was I embarrassed! Talk about learning lessons in life! There's another one!

Helen and I decided we had better skip a night so her parents didn't get suspicious but the following night when I picked her up, <u>I could tell by the look on their faces that they knew! They knew what was going on!</u> Now, I assume they knew because they knew their daughter had hot pants and I was the next one in line to benefit from it. So I got the stares and withstood their frowns and we moved out.

This night I decided to use my own car knowing that somehow we would find a way to get the deed done. After all, where there is a will there is a way, right? Now picture this! For some reason, I decided to go park in the village dump. I guess I reasoned that nobody would be dumping anything at night, so it would probably be a good hiding spot. You see, my car was a bright red roadster with wide whitewall tires and stood out like an elephant turd on an ant- hill and e-vv-e-r-y-b-o-d-y within 20 miles knew who owned it! Well, I lucked out, nobody came to the dump that night. It's a good thing because if they had, they would have been presented with quite an unforgettable scene. "Ole one duck Lovett" had found some new game and he wasn't shooting bullets. In order to accommodate the situation of no back seat and a steering wheel in the way, not to mention the floor mounted gear shift, I had to open both doors, put the top down, and hang out both sides of the car at the same time. A snap shot of that would have made the funny papers for a hundred miles around!

The next day Helen went back to Ohio. We promised to stay in touch by phone and get together at least once a month. As it worked out, it was somehow never convenient to visit one another. We spoke on the phone a few times but things seemed to get tense with her. About three months from our parting, I called her one Saturday afternoon and she" **shocked"** me with the dreaded statement no young stud wants to hear! <u>"Guess what? I'm pregnant!"</u> That's the scariest thing ever to a young guy and I nearly fell off the stool in the phone booth I was using. Because of that fear, I had always used protection and I was dumbfounded! I said, "that's impossible!" to which she replied, "no! it's not," and it happened! She then pleaded with me to come to Ohio and marry her. "My dad will buy you a new car and also pay for the balance of your education." My head was spinning and I said, "I'll call you back" but before I could hang up the phone, she said, "My mother is here, would you like to talk to her?" Now what a stupid question that was! Her mother was certainly the last one I wanted to talk to, and I replied "no thanks," and hung up the phone.

My life had just turned upside down! I had big plans to finish college and then play professional baseball. A wife and a kid simply would not fit into the scheme of things. I did a lot of thinking the next few days, and the more I thought about it, the more I began to believe that if she was pregnant, I was not the father. I figured the real culprit didn't measure up to either her or her parents and I was going to be the "fall guy"! I was ambitious. I was attending college, came from a nice family, had a promising future and they just decided I would be the one.

The following weekend, I called her and asked to meet her somewhere so we could talk privately and without undue pressure from her parents. She didn't like that idea. She demurred and wanted a yes or no answer before we met. In my mind, her answer confirmed my suspicions and I said, "no! I will not marry you now!" We said "goodbye" and that was the last time I ever spoke to her.

Although I played for Alden the next summer, Helen and her family did not come to that area and vacation that year. But an interesting thing happened a couple of years later. My brother and I stopped at the Clam River bar for lunch and a friend of mine was there and said "I saw your old girlfriend the other day." "She had a little blond baby boy with her." I nearly choked on my sandwich! To my knowledge, nobody else knew about the closeness of our relationship and to this day, I still have my doubts. The way I see it, if it was my child, my whereabouts have never been difficult for anyone to trace and no one has ever sought me out and said, "you are my father!"

Loyds wife, Martha, was something else. She wasn't much of a looker but she was very smart and took good care of Loyd, with one notable exception. Not long after my little escapade with Helen, Martha and I were alone in their house one day and the witch propositioned me! She was about 15 years older than me but I guess that just doesn't make much difference when it comes to sex. <u>Older women do like younger men!</u> Look at all of these female school-teachers having sex with their students. By the way, I don't understand the public outcry on that issue at all. All the young guys I knew would give their right arm to have sex with one or more of their teachers! And it certainly would not have a bad physiological affect on them. At that young age, guys will hump nearly anything that will hold still and not give it a second thought! The do-gooders, who call this an outrage, are just jealous and frustrated that they aren't personally involved themselves.

Getting back to Martha, to say her proposition surprised me, would be an understatement. It was not as though she wasn't getting any. Although Loyd was a paraplegic, he was still able to perform sexually. Perhaps Martha wanted to try someone who had full movement of all of their body parts, or just someone younger. Who knows! Whatever her motivation, I wasn't enticed, and said "no." Also, I wouldn't be a party to cheating on Loyd. I was a guest in his house and had better morals than that. A few years later though, I learned he didn't share the moral fiber I was raised with.

Loyd and Martha had a winter cottage down by Lakeland, Florida. He was managing a class D professional baseball team there and they asked me to come down, join the team and live with them again. I agreed and while there I met a lovely Hispanic girl who worked at the local drug store. She was 9 years older than me and had a sixteen year- old daughter who was just as beautiful as her mother. Loyalty still meant a lot to me and although the daughter flirted with me, I was true to her mother, Anna. Anna was a hot-blooded gal and we shared some great times together. One evening when I picked her up for a date, she told me that Loyd had been in the drug store earlier and hit on her. His line was that he was older than me and had " <u>more experience"</u>! She was mortified and although Loyd had been a good friend of hers, she was completely turned off by his proposition and asked me to tell him to stay away from her. I, too, was shocked that Loyd would have such little regard for me to do such a thing. I called him out on it when Martha wasn't around and he wasn't the least embarrassed by the whole thing. His arrogance disgusted me and I packed up and left! Luckily, I had several buddies on the team that were willing to share an apartment with me and I moved in with one of them. I lost all respect for Loyd for that, and wanted to tell him about Martha's proposition to me, but thought better of it. I actually gained a little respect back for Martha because of the incident. It wasn't long after that, that I quit the team and went to play for the St. Petersburg Saints in the Florida International league. But that is another whole story I will save for another day. For now, back to Bellaire.

Village Dump

Chapter Twenty Seven:
"Cooning" Watermelons

I have no idea where that expression comes from, but I expect it may be a racial slur. Anyway, that's what it was called at the time and in keeping with the truth of the story, I will go with it here.

The fall of the year was one of my favorite times in Bellaire. It is the mystical time when nights are cool, the moon is big, and young men's hormones take over their bodies to do something exciting! Bill Crandall drove this model A Ford coupe and after basketball practice one evening, Bill, Lyle, Carl Griffith and I had a yearning for some fresh watermelon. Rumor was, there was a farmer who lived about 4 miles NE of town who owned a large watermelon patch that was close to a dirt road behind his farm. So, after dark we all piled in to Bill's model A and cruised out of town. There was only room for 2 inside the car so Lyle and Carl rode in the open-air rumble seat in the rear. Carl knew how to locate the field, thank Heaven, because it was an overcast night with no moon to light the way. We parked the car in some bushes off of the road so as not to cause suspicion if anyone came around and we walked toward the field in the pitch-black darkness of the night. A short ways in we encountered a 5- foot barbed wire fence and at the edge of the melon-patch field, was a ten foot wide drainage ditch we needed to navigate as well. The melon-patch lay about 50 yards beyond the ditch. The melons were huge and ripe and we each began to pick one when all-of-a sudden, a bright light was turned on us, a door slammed and here come two big, barking, snarling dogs! <u>We hadn't counted on this!</u> We dropped the heavy melons in our tracks and took off as fast as we could towards the car. Did I mention that Bill Crandall was chicken and stayed in the car while the rest of us did the dirty work? He used the excuse that someone might steal or break into his prized automobile. Now give me a break! There probably weren't ten cars that came down that road in a year, and besides, who would want that old junker of his? But anyway, he stayed behind. So there were just the three of us. We were all good athletes but after about three steps, it was clearly apparent who was the fastest in a flight of fear! I was "a-picken-em-up and layin-em down!" It was pitch dark but when I got to where I thought the ditch was, I gave one huge leap and cleared the whole thing in one bound. Behind me I heard a "splat-splat" and I knew Lyle and Carl had not been so lucky and found the bottom of the ditch instead. The dogs were getting louder, the farmer was yelling and I was as scared as I had ever been! As I approached the road, I could faintly see Bill's car in the distance and I took a quick guess as to about where the fence was and on the dead run I gave another tremendous leap and cleared it completely without a scratch. I heard a "twang-twang" behind me and realized Carl and Lyle had both hit the fence. At that point, I figured they would get caught for sure so I scrambled into the car and said to Bill **"take off"** because Lyle and Carl were toast! Bill's eyes were big as saucers, he let out the clutch, hit the gas and we barreled down the road. After we had gone about a mile, my conscience got the best of me and I said to Bill," you know, I just assumed they were caught because the dogs were right on our heels, but maybe we should go back and make sure." Bill turned around and about half a mile back, sure enough, there they were jogging in the road and gasping for air. Their clothes were torn and muddy and for some reason, they were very "pissed off"! By some miracle, they had managed to escape the ditch, the fence and the dogs and didn't appreciate us not waiting for them! I guess when the farmer got to the ditch, he figured he had successfully defended his melons and called off his dogs, which were about to nip the butts off my buddies. I apologized for bailing on them and we all had a good laugh about it on the way home (sans melons).

Well that was enough "melon- cooning" for me but not for Lyle. He really liked watermelons. So, a few nights later, when he and I were "out on the town", he said, "I know of a melon patch right here on the north side of town close to the railroad track." "What say we give it a try?" I said, no thanks, you go ahead, I'm going on home". As we parted, I secretly had an idea to play a little prank on my friend! Good-natured pranks were common in those days. Remember, we had no television or Internet to entertain us, so we had to manufacture our own fun, and we did a bang-up job of it.

As we went our separate ways and I was far enough away so that Lyle couldn't see me in the darkness of the night, I retraced my steps but stayed a safe distance behind him so he had no knowledge of my presence. When he reached the melon patch, I carefully worked my way behind him and as he headed down the railroad tracks with melons under both arms, I began running hard towards him, yelling loud and flailing my arms like an angry farmer. I faked my voice and hollered <u>"Hey you thief, drop those melons"</u>! Lyle was a fairly good runner, but not nearly as fast as I was, but I must have scared the crap out of him because he dropped both melons and ran like a bat-out-of-hell down the tracks toward town! He ran so fast, I could barely out-run him and when he finally gave up and turned around to accept his fate, I was completely out of breath. As I got closer to him I started to laugh and he instantly realized he had been HAD! And he was pissed! His anger didn't last long as we walked back up the tracks to salvage the biggest pieces of the melons. As I recall, they weren't even that good. They hadn't fully ripened yet to be tasty, so it was all for naught.

Years later, Lyle had a similar experience when he was working for the railroad. He was a station agent for the C&O and was working night duty. He noticed a railroad car on a siding close to the station that was full of huge watermelons and he figured no one would miss a couple of those beauties so when no one was looking he went to the open door on the car and crawled in. He grabbed two of the big melons, one under each arm and jumped back down to the tracks. In his eagerness to pull off the heist, he forgot one thing - <u>the weight of the melons!</u> When his feet hit the ground, so did the melons as they slipped from his greedy grasp. They splattered all over the ground and he was so disappointed, he felt like crying. Poor Lyle, his weakness for free melons came back to bite him again.

Chapter Twenty Eight:
Dick Anger and Al Kundrick

One of the benefits of my "steady" relationship with Nancy, was getting to know her great family and their friends. Nancy's parents were beautiful people in all senses of the word. They were wonderful to me and treated me as their son-in-law even though we were not close to the marriage stage in our lives. They liked me and I liked them and they had begun to make plans for Nancy and I to take over their business as soon as we were married. They would have been perfect in-laws for me.

Nancy had an older brother, Dick, with a fantastic personality and we became instant good friends. Now anyone with good life experiences knows that people are attracted to others who have the same qualities and likenesses as themselves, thus Dick had some remarkable friends that I had the pleasure of getting to know as well.

Dick had established his life with his beautiful wife, Sonja back in the Redford area of Detroit and had remained there when his parents moved to Bellaire. His best friend was a handsome, "Lil-Abner" look-alike named Al Kundrick who would often accompany Dick and Sonja when they visited his parents in Bellaire.

One summer day when they were all in town, Al asked me to take him fishing in my boat on the upper(Intermediate) river, above the spillway. I was elated at the suggestion, not only because I loved to fish, but because Al, whom I admired, had asked me to take him. The river there above the railroad bridge and the spillway was thriving with fish, mostly Bass, Pike and pan-fish. We began to troll, my favorite method of fishing, traveling upstream against the current and it was just a few minutes until I got a "strike," and my line began to bob! By the time I had stopped the boat and grabbed my line, there was no doubt that I had a big fish on. We hadn't brought a net so we decided to beach the boat and haul the fish in to shore. For those of you who like to fish, you know there is nothing more thrilling than to have a big fish on with light tackle! The fish will fight and take the line on a run and you must be very careful not to resist too strongly or you could break the line and lose the fish. Then, when he tires a little, you reel him back until he regains his strength and runs again. This procedure is repeated again and again until he has finally tired enough to reel him all of the way in. When I finally landed this fish on the shore, I realized he was a magnificent Grass-Pike of about 10 lbs and was very angry with me. I could see it in his eyes! For the moment, he was docile. Now you might think that for all the fishing I did, I would have all the proper equipment necessary for catching fish of all sizes. The truth is, I had never caught one this big! I fished primarily on the river for small Rock-Bass and Sunfish and the occasional Small-mouth Bass. Yes, I had a net that I rarely used and a gaff-hook that I had never had the occasion to use so I didn't bring them with me either. Now I had a problem! How was I going to get the hook out of his mouth without getting bit by those sharp teeth that Pike are so famous for? Al said, "just grab his head with your left hand and take out the hook with your right". Notice here that Al didn't offer to help. He hadn't seen a fish this big ever, and because of his lack of experience with the sport he wasn't willing to sacrifice one of his own hands as a learning experience either. It was my fish, so I had to do what had to be done! Carefully, I took hold of the head with my left hand but it was difficult to handle because it was so slippery. As I began to try to dislodge the barbed hook, the angry fish saw his chance for revenge and began to thrash as wildly as he could! "Ooow! I hollered as that Pike successfully <u>transferred</u> the large barbed hook from his mouth to, and through the forefinger on my right hand.

To this day, as I sit here and type this paragraph, I look at my finger with the telltale scar and I re-live the pain of it all, and the memory of the angry look on that fish's face. Yes, we ate him many years ago, but he left a legacy with me that I will never forget. Nor will I forget Al and what he did in an attempt to correct the painful situation I was in. We had no way to cut the barb off of the hook, so Al just took my hand and pulled the damn hook back through my finger! Talk about pain! <u>Try that sometime</u>! That had to be compared to torture by pulling your nails out with a "pliers!" You never know how much pain you can endure until you experience it. In spite of all of that, Al was still my friend. He did what he thought was best and I appreciated his compassion for me at the time, even if I disagree with his methodology. As you can guess, when he pulled the barb out, it took a lot of the meat from my finger with it and I began to bleed profusely. Al wrapped my finger in a handkerchief and by the time we got home it had stopped bleeding. He drove me to good old "Doc Rogers" to get my wound dressed and a Tetanus shot, which only added to my pain, but as witnessed by this book, I managed to live through it all. Al was a great guy but he sure <u>sucked</u> as a surgeon! We were good friends for many years and to the best of my knowledge, for some reason, he never married even though he would have made some deserving woman a good husband.

That fall, Dick and Al came back to town one weekend and asked me to take them hunting. They didn't have licenses and didn't want to spend the money as it was only to be a one- day thing. To alleviate our fears about getting caught without licenses, I decided to take them with me on our own private 260- acre property where there wasn't a chance of being stopped by a game warden. We took Dick's new Ford sedan and he parked it at the end of a lane on open land close to the woods. We were hunting small game so I gave them each one of my shotguns and I chose my favorite small-bore 25/20 Winchester lever-action rifle that I was very accurate with.

Our hunt was unsuccessful that day for lack of game and on the way back to the car, I began to brag about my superior marksmanship with the gun I was carrying. I said I could take the eye out of a squirrel at 100 yards. Dick decided to challenge my bragging claims and proposed an offer I couldn't refuse. "I'll bet you my car to your one dollar that you can't hit the ball on the end of my car aerial from here." He said. "you are on!" I replied as I got down on one knee to steady my shot.(You already know the answer to this story, don't you?) Well here is how it plays out. At that distance with my excellent eyesight, I could see the aerial but not the ball on the end of it. It was only the size of a pencil eraser and I could see where it probably should be, but I could not see it perfectly. Add on the fact that there was a little breeze moving the aerial slightly and affecting the bullet, it was an impossible shot no matter how good I thought I was. So I took careful aim with the open sight, allowing for the drop angle and windage and carefully squeezed the trigger! <u>P-I-N-G! went the aerial as it bounced back and forth from the impact!</u> There were four of us there watching this spectacle and we all looked at each other with open-mouthed astonishment. I tried to look cool as I reached out my hand for Dick's car keys. Poor Dick, he didn't know what to do. He didn't want to be known as a welsher, but on the other hand, he wasn't about to give me his car. So he said. "Now wait a minute, we know you hit the aerial, but did you hit the ball?" "Let's go and look at it". We trudged up to the car to take a careful look at the aerial and sure enough, there was a lead colored imprint directly on the side of the aerial ball facing the direction of the shot. Again, he was flabbergasted and didn't know what to say. I could have probably played the scenario out and demanded the car, but of course, I couldn't do that. I knew it was a one-in-a-million lucky shot and relinquished my claim, much to Dick's relief. At that point in time, Dick and Al now believed they were in the company of the world's greatest marksman and they looked at me with a new respect in their eyes! And you know what? I thought I was a pretty darn good marksman too! It was quite a story to tell to Dick and Nancy's parents when we returned.

Chapter Twenty Nine: Michigan State

In the fall of 1950 after graduation from Bellaire high school, my life changed dramatically as it usually does for any student when they begin this new era in their life. My 5 years in Bellaire had been so enjoyable that I was still on cloud nine and it was inconceivable to imagine that the future could be any different for me. But it was! When a child reaches maturity and steps out in the world on his own without the comforts of home and the protection of his parents, it can be a scary thing and suddenly I was a bit apprehensive. On the positive side, I was eager to attend college and obtain a life enhancing degree or better yet, excel in collegiate sports and pursue a professional baseball career. On the other hand, I had to leave Nancy, the love of my life, and all of the friends I had made during the last five years. Yes, I could come back home on the weekends and see them, but it wouldn't be the same. And sure enough, it wasn't. To make matters worse, my parents sold our house and moved back to the Detroit area again and all of that had a disastrous effect on my psyche and personal "well-being!" I was no longer in the comfort zone of my home and personal friends and it took a toll on my confidence as to who I was and where I fit in to the scheme of things at that time in my life. In high school, I knew everybody and everybody knew me or who I was. Now in college, there were thousands of students and hundreds of good athletes and suddenly <u>I was just a number!</u> It created a challenge for me that I was a little bit uncomfortable with. Was I up to it?

I did have one advantage that gave me a running start at Michigan State. I was there on an athletic scholarship for baseball so the coaching staff was quite aware of my past high school accomplishments and they wasted no time in bringing me in to their program.

Before I left Bellaire, Nancy and I had a long talk and realizing the constraints of the coming distance between us, we had agreed on an amicable split so we could date other people but promised to spend as many weekends with each other as reasonably possible. Another reason for doing this is so that we could test our real commitments to each other after pursuing other interests until I came back from college. It was a mistake! It turned out to be a complete disaster for me and if I had that one decision to make again in my life, I would have done it differently. Yes, I dated some other girls in college, but Nancy still had my heart and I expected she would share the same feelings because we had been together for so long. After about six months of this arrangement, Nancy wanted out. I was heartbroken and it took me a long time to get over it. Because of my athletic prowess, I was becoming a BMOC (big man on campus) at Michigan State, but it was in my world only now and not in Nancy's. Michigan State news was not an everyday thing in the little town of Bellaire. As I recall, my baseball accomplishments did not even make it back to the Bellaire Record newspaper as a "home town boy" normally would. In retrospect, because my parents had moved away, there was no one there to sing my praises to the paper and in reality, I was no longer a "home town boy". There was another harsh "life lesson" in this experience for me. It may sound mean and perhaps even selfish. And it certainly isn't the honorable thing to do, but it is profoundly reality! If you love the girl and she loves you, have sex with her when the opportunity presents itself. Don't be the "nice guy" and put it off till marriage. Sex nails it down. It establishes a definite commitment from the girl that she cannot escape from as long as the boy is not abusive or abhorrent in some other way. I did not demand this commitment from Nancy and it cost me a lifetime with the true love of my life.

It all started one weekend when I came home from State with the intention of spending some quality time with Nancy. My parents had not moved yet so I borrowed dad's car and went to pick her up. When I got to Nancy's house her parents told me she had gone out on an early date with Joe Conroy but promised to be home by 10 PM to meet me. Needless to say, I was a bit peeved that she would do this to me, when she knew I would be home and looking for her. I left her house and returned at 10:15 to pick her up only to find that she still wasn't home. Now I was angry! I went back into town and soon discovered Joe's car driving slowly towards Nancy's house. They saw me and as I made a u-turn to follow them, Joe slowed his car to a mere crawl to intentionally aggravate me. I guess he didn't know how angry I could get and he picked the wrong time to find out. I pulled right up to his bumper and when he slowed even more, I just rammed his car with mine. That produced instant results and when he opened his door and his feet hit the ground, my right fist caught him flat in the face and broke his nose. He staggered back bleeding like a stuck pig and the fight was over. I felt redemption but as I turned to Nancy for understanding, I ran into a buzz saw. She was angry with me! How could that be? She was my girl and I had just saved her from an outside obnoxious suitor. Or had I? But she was angry knowing full well I would be angry that she had not been home waiting for me. At that very moment I realized the truth of the matter. It was over between us and our relationship would never be the same again. And to make matters worse my right hand began to swell up and get very painful. I had hit Joe so hard I broke a bone in my hand and my college baseball career would have to wait 6 months for a re-start. So that was it! The beginning of the end! Nancy and I would date a few times again but we would never put it all together. We remained friends until I received a letter from her one day telling me she was getting married to a fellow she had met at work. It hit me hard, I was devastated that I had lost her!

The fellow Nancy married turned out to be a great guy and they raised a nice family together. About a year ago, I heard that she was very ill and didn't have long to live. She and her family had moved back to northern Michigan South of Traverse City. I finally located her phone number and was able to speak with her a few moments for the last time. We reminisced about the good times we had together and then said our goodbyes. To this day, I am saddened by her passing and still grieve for her. You were a wonderful girl Nancy! Rest in piece in God's great Kingdom!

When the baseball coach at Michigan State discovered I had a broken hand, he was furious with me. My accident was just before the start of the season of my sophomore year and I wasn't able to pitch until the following year. I had had an outstanding year as a freshman and the coach was looking forward to my being the pillar of his pitching staff. His name was John Kobbs and was well acclaimed for his ability to produce collegiate stars that went on to play professional ball. So my little scenario put a damper on his plans for that season.

In the fall of 1950, I lived on campus and shared a room with my high-school buddy, Jack Matthew in East-Shaw Hall dormitory. At that time there were no co-ed dorms so East-Shaw was strictly men only. There were several other northern Michigan students lodged there and one of them was Don Cutler from East Jordan. Don was attending on a football scholarship and had been a star player on a great championship team there. They were coached by the now famous, "Dan Devine". I had met Dan after a practice basketball game Bellaire had with East Jordan. He liked the way I played and sought me out after the game to tell me so. We became friends and I would see him several times again at Michigan State where he had later moved to advance his career as an assistant coach. I also met Don Cutler at Shaw Hall and we struck up a good friendship because of our mutual sports interests. Don and I even cut a tawdry vocal record together of "Goodnight Irene" in a small, recording booth that some enterprising organization had placed in dorms around the campus. "Don, if you ever read this book, I still have that old vinyl record". Both Don and I had girlfriends back home in northern Michigan at the time and one weekend we decided to hitchhike home and surprise them. Hitchhiking was still a common activity back then and not considered dangerous at all. Nancy and I even hitched a ride from East Lansing to Detroit one time without incident. Little did Don and I know though, this time would be different! We bummed a ride from East Lansing to US 27 north of Lansing on Friday afternoon from a friend and stuck out our thumbs for a ride north. About ten minutes later a car with two young men in their twenties stopped and gave us a lift. We thanked them for their kindness and piled into the back seat. They inquired as to where we were from and where we were headed and after a short conversation, we all settled in for the ride. Some time later the front seat passenger produced a bottle of whiskey and they proceeded to have a few snorts. They politely offered us a drink but staying true to our athletic backgrounds, we both declined.

As I recall, it was about the middle of September and the days were getting shorter so that darkness came upon us as we approached the town of Grayling. Our hosts were pretty well oiled by then and to our surprise they exited the highway and began driving down a desolate dirt road into the state forest. Without saying a word, the passenger opened the glove compartment and produced a hand-gun. Don and I looked at each other apprehensively but said nothing. We realized we were completely at the mercy of these two strangers if they decided to take advantage of us for whatever purpose. All of a sudden, the man with the gun shouted, "there goes one!" as a doe deer crossed the road in front of the car. He opened his window and pumped several shots at the deer as it bounded away through the trees.

Obviously, deer season had not started yet, and even if it had, it was unlawful to hunt at night with a light, and also unlawful to shoot a doe deer without a special license. <u>Don and I quickly realized we were in the hands of lawbreakers who had the capacity and the means to be violent!</u> We were both physically fit and in a fair fight we could take care of ourselves but we were no match for drunken lunatics with a gun, so we had good reason to be apprehensive! By some miracle, the excitement of shooting at the deer seemed to momentarily satisfy our host's need for further violent activity. They turned the car around and drove into Grayling where they stopped at the first bar. They said they would have a couple of drinks and then would drive us on into our destination of Gaylord. We all entered the bar and when they were looking the other way and the opportunity presented itself, Don and I high-tailed it out of the door and down the street! In retrospect, I think this was one of the best decisions I have ever made in my life. "Who knows what might have happened if we had stayed and waited in that bar?" We found the Greyhound bus station and took the first bus north to Gaylord. While in the station, we called our friends at home and made arrangements for them to pick us up at the bus station, where we were finally safe but with a very hairy story to tell! I don't know who those men were, or what their intentions were, but they gave us a pretty good scare! After our initial conversation, they were quite tight-lipped and never gave us a clue as to who they were, what their occupation was or where they were going. I think Don and I were quite fortunate in making our escape at the time we did. We had an Angel looking over us that Friday evening in September of 1950. Hitchhiking can be a fun adventure, but it can also be a bad idea! It was rather fun a couple of other times. In my sophomore high-school year, Lyle and I decided to alter our summer-time boredom by hitchhiking to Detroit. My parents were spending a couple of weeks there in a friend's house in the suburb of Royal-Oak while they spent the same amount of time at our house in Bellaire. "Kind of an early-age time-share thing". Lyle had a girl friend in Midland, Michigan named Marcy Brown. Her parents had vacationed in the Bellaire area a couple of times and Lyle met her on the tennis courts. She was a pretty girl with long blonde hair and Lyle hadn't seen her in a while so he and I decided to hitchhike to Royal Oak via Midland. We figured it would be a good adventure and "life-training" experience.

We set out early one morning with clean thumbs and big smiles to "do our thing" and learn about life as hitchhiking bums! As I recall, the first part of the trip was not too bad except that it took us about four hours to get to Midland. Lyle spent a couple of hours with Marcie, and I, with nothing to do, just hung around and killed time. I felt a bit out of place and was embarrassed that I was "in the way," so to speak, of their apparent desire to be alone. After a couple of hours I was finally able to pry the two apart so that Lyle and I could be on our way again. Some time later, when we finally arrived in the Detroit area, "hitching" became more difficult and we were only able to get to within 5 miles of our destination. I tried to call my parents to come and get us but they were not at home so we began to walk, and walk, and walk! Remember, we had already spent a good share of the day walking and hitching and our feet began to violently object to the abuse we were giving them. At that age and time, footwear wasn't apparently as important as it is now. "Walking shoes" had not been invented yet and the ones we were wearing objected to the use we were putting them to. So we took them off and continued on our bare feet. I was finally able to reach my mother at the house but she couldn't come to get us because dad had dropped her off there and taken the car on another errand. She gave us directions to the house and we limped home some time later. Needless to say, we didn't go walking for a couple of days.

The next morning, my parents had already gone out for the day when we dragged our butts out of bead, but before we could get up, my little brother, "Bud" came running into our bedroom and yelled, <u>"Klooney got out and I can't find her!!"</u> Now <u>"Klooney"</u> was out host family's dog. She was a cute little Beagle mix and mother had left strict instructions with Bud that she could only be taken out on her leash. Beagles are hunting dogs by nature and they will follow their nose all day long to hell and gone without a leash. Evidently Bud forgot his instructions or just didn't want to bother with the leash, but whatever, she took off and didn't come back. "What should I do?" Bud asked. I was still half asleep and I told Bud to get me the phone book and he could call the local dog pound and alert them to be on the lookout for her. Bud was only about eleven at the time and although not the least bit intimidated by any task, he was not the most proficiently skilled in matters of this nature! We hadn't had a family dog of our own since he was a baby. I found the number of the dog pound for him and told him to call them and see if Klooney had turned up there yet. As Lyle and I still lounged in our bed we heard Bud dial the number on the phone in the hallway and simply say, "Is Klooney there? She's a Spiegel!" Lyle and I rolled with laughter, as Bud said disgustedly, "they hung up on me!" "I guess I dialed the wrong number." <u>I'll say one thing for my little brother, nothing bothered him!</u> Right or wrong, he would wade in with both feet and get the job done, whatever it took. I convinced him to wait until I was dressed and I would take care of the problem. We couldn't find the dog but later that day, someone found her, read her dog tag with the address on it and returned her to us.

In the summer of 1951, between my freshman and sophomore years at college, I purchased the shell of an old automobile from a good friend of mine back in St. Clair Shores. "Bobby" Miron had a 1936 Ford roadster that he had tried to soup up into a "hot-rod" by adding a 4 barrel "carb" and other refinements. The old Ford engine roared a lot but it never achieved the performance Bobby was looking for, so he sold it to me for $75.00. It was my first car and although I was happy to get it, I wasn't into the hot-rod thing and I had to do some extensive rehabilitating before I would drive it. I certainly didn't want to take it back to college to show my friends until it was presentable. The "thing" was all stripped down with no fenders, no top, no bumpers, no headlights and no upholstery except for a torn leather seat. It was only a two-seater except for a rumble seat compartment instead of a trunk at the back of the car. It took me the whole summer as I went from junk- yard to junk- yard across the state to locate parts for it. After I finally found the necessary parts, the big job of rehabilitation began. I installed bumpers, fenders, corduroy upholstery, (thanks to Martha Ammisegger who did the sewing for me), and a continental wheel kit on the back of the rumble seat. Actually, that is where the spare tire is located, and then I painted the whole thing "fire-engine" red. After that I drove it to Detroit and had a new black, canvas top installed. I couldn't afford new white-wall tires so I purchased a quart of rubberized white paint and painted on the white walls. Young as I was, I was a perfectionist and I must say I did a hell of a job because you absolutely could not tell those white-walls were painted on! When I finished the job, I drove it over to the Miron's house where I had bought the car and Bobby's dad refused to believe me that they were painted on! He got down on his hands and knees to look closer and still didn't believe it. He went to his grave several years later not believing it. When he got to heaven he certainly knew the truth and I expect to hear an apology whispered in my ear some day before I pass on. He may be waiting until I get to heaven to tell me, assuming I will make it, but what if I don't? I guess I won't worry about it. The important thing is I ended up with one "classy looking" roadster and I was the envy of all of my fraternity brothers at State.

During my sophomore college year, Nancy had graduated from high school and was living and working in Muskegon. We were still close friends and while talking to her on the phone one evening, she told me she was going to take a bus to Detroit the following weekend to visit her cousins in Redford. I said to her, "don't do that Nancy, I will come to Muskegon on Friday night, take you to a movie and then drive you to Detroit on Saturday in my shiny new "roadster".

She thought that was a great idea so we proceeded with the plan. She lived in a small apartment with another girl and there was no room for me there, so she got me a cheap room in the local YMCA for the night. Everything went smooth until we started to leave Muskegon on Saturday morning. We were driving down a narrow street past a spot where a 16 wheeler had stopped to unload a package. It was in the opposite lane of traffic and as I began to pass it another car came towards me also to pass the truck and he pulled into my lane. I obviously had the right-of-way but he kept right on a – coming! I had no choice but to just stop, as I had nowhere to go to get out of his way. Well, he kept on coming and hit us head-on! Luckily, he wasn't going very fast so no one was hurt. The grille on my car was smashed, the bumper bent and water gushed from my radiator. The truck driver was our witness and couldn't believe the man didn't stop! As we found out, the other driver was an old man and didn't even have any brakes on his car! He apologized meekly to me, gave me his name, address and phone number and drove off. He seemed like a nice guy and here is where I learned another life-lesson! I didn't have enough sense to take his license plate number and found out later he had given me false information. He probably didn't even have a driver's license so I was on my own to get my car repaired. Did I feel stupid! There went our plans for a fun weekend trip to Detroit!

Nancy was upset but I said not to worry, I would find a way to resolve the problem. I was able to temporarily patch the radiator to where it only had a small leak and with a couple of one-gallon jugs filled with water, we chugged back to my frat house in East Lansing. By then I realized the beat-up roadster wouldn't make it to Detroit so I came up with another brilliant idea! <u>We would hitchhike to Detroit!</u> It was a crazy idea but Nancy loved it! One of my frat brothers gave us a lift to East Grand River Ave. and we stuck out our thumbs. It wasn't long when a nice young couple in a new Oldsmobile stopped and inquired as to where we were going. We told them " Detroit" and they said, "hop in, we are going there too." The young woman was driving and she was a bit apprehensive about the idea but her husband said, "don't worry about it honey, this young couple are in need of a ride and we will be happy to help them out." The ride was pleasant and uneventful except for one little incident. <u>This woman had a heavy foot!</u> It must have been made of lead from her knee down. She drove so fast that at one point she came up behind another car that was going the speed limit and she panicked! She hit the brakes so hard it almost put us all through the windshield. Remember, there were no seat belts back then. This woman grabbed the steering wheel with both hands and screamed, <u>"Oh Sid, what is it?"</u> At that moment Nancy and I looked at each other and came to the realization that this woman was just learning to drive!

Hence her previous apprehension about giving us a ride came full circle into play and now we were the apprehensive ones! Thank God, the rest of the ride was smooth and the nice people dropped us off at my parent's house in Novi. I used my dad's car to take Nancy to her cousin's house and that was the last hitchhiking adventure in my life. It is too dangerous now-a-days and intelligent people with a choice just don't chance it anymore.

Chapter Thirty:
Doctor Rodgers

There is no way I can complete this book without reference to Dr. John Rodgers. Over the course of one's lifetime you meet a few extraordinary people who touch your life in such a positive way that you can never forget them. Dr. Rodgers was one such man! If the town of Bellaire was a great little town in the 1950's, he was a major contributor to that mystique. Kind, gentle and compassionate, he was also deeply religious but not to a fault. John was understanding and considerate of every individual's situation, whatever it may be and he did his best to improve upon it. No matter if you were rich or poor, or what your status was in the community, he made house calls when you needed him. Now-a-days, most well trained and well educated doctors are very eager to charge large fees accordingly in order to finance a lifestyle far above the average citizen in their area.

John had all of the good qualities and then some but not the greed. His fees were extremely low and he lived in town with his family in a quaint little house that also served as his office and his life was dedicated to serving his community.

I recall one Sunday afternoon in the seventies. I had married and moved my family back to Bellaire in order to raise my children in the same decent environment I had been so fortunate to grow up in. I drove my family to the Lake Michigan Beach at Eastport to picnic and swim. My son, Tracy, accidentally cut his foot severely on a broken beer bottle some fool had thrown in the water. So Sally, my wife, and I wrapped his foot in a towel as tightly as we could and drove the 20 some miles back to Bellaire because we knew that Sunday or not, Dr. Rodgers would be available to do whatever was necessary to treat him. That treatment included multiple stitches, shots for pain and Tetanus and even crutches for a few days. And the bill for all of this skill and care on a Sunday afternoon? <u>Ten dollars!</u> Can you believe that? Now I had a good business in town and could afford whatever he chose to charge me, but $10.00 is all he would take. I said to him, "Doc, I can't believe this is all you are charging me." "If I had known this, I would have brought my dog to you last weekend. He got into a porcupine and I had to take him to the vet to take the quills out. His fee was $27.00 and he didn't have half the work you did." Doc Rodgers just smiled as he always did and said. "Thanks Bill, I appreciate your business."

Another time when I was 15 years old, I was very physically active during the summer vacation from school. I awakened early one Sunday morning and met my buddies at the Bellaire Golf Course for 18 holes of golf before a baseball game I had to pitch at 1:00 PM. After golf I went home, showered, ate lunch and was at the ball park at a quarter past twelve to warm up and then pitched a nine inning game. This was not high school ball but an independent recreation league for players age 15 to 40 or so. During the game I noticed a stinging sensation just above my right elbow. I had developed a small red pimple there about the size of a pinhead. It didn't bother me that much so I didn't pay much attention to it at that time and after the game I returned home to shower again and eat dinner. That evening I joined Lyle for a couple of sets of tennis like we always did on Sunday evenings. Later on, the pain increased and my elbow started to swell up like a balloon! The next day it was worse so I went to see Doc Rodgers. Unfortunately, Doc happened to be out of town at a medical convention and wouldn't return until Thursday. His nurse, Barbara Joe Thumb, looked at my elbow with a worried look on her face and told me to go to Munson hospital in Traverse City immediately! We didn't know it at the time, of course, but what I had was a "staff infection" now called

MRSA. She said I had a serious infection and it needed to be tended to ASAP! Munson hospital had a specialist on staff there and he could better assess the situation. Dad took me there in his pickup truck and they took me right in for observation. I suddenly became aware that everyone there who looked at my arm had very solemn looks on their faces and it began to worry me! The staff doctor gingerly examined my arm then talked to dad in the other room where I could not hear the conversation! In a few minutes, dad emerged and said, "come on Bill, let's go home!" As we walked out, I inquired as to what the doctor had said but dad wouldn't tell me. Now I was worried! He was very quiet and obviously concerned as we drove home. I kept asking him what the problem was and when he could no longer keep his silence, he blurted out, "they want to amputate your arm! Otherwise, the infection will spread until it kills you!" I was aghast! I had some close calls in my fifteen years of life, but nothing like this! There was the time when at 4 years old, I was playing in our garage and got my head caught between dad's trailer and the workbench. I was just hanging there by my head and unable to move or touch the ground. Finally, my mother heard my screams and came to my rescue. Then when I was six, I accidentally swallowed an ice cube and got it caught in my throat, cutting off my air supply. Dad was there that time and saved me by turning me upside down and pounding on my back until he dislodged the ice cube and I cheated death yet again.

This time though, was different! I told dad not to let them take my arm and I would rather take my chances on dying. He agreed and we went home to await Dr. Rodgers return on Thursday. I don't know why, but I had complete faith in Dr. Rodgers. I was confident he would know what to do to save my life.

Early Thursday morning there was a knock at our door and it was Doc. He was standing there with a huge smile on his face like he always did and was carrying his little black bag and he looked like an angel to me. With a chuckle in his voice, he strode in and said, "let's have a look at that arm." He asked mother to get some clean towels and a bowl of hot steaming water and I could tell by the confidence in his voice, he knew what he was dealing with. He laid my arm on a wet towel, put both hands around my arm, one above the red spot and one below and said, "this is going to hurt a bit, but you can bear it." He began to squeeze my swollen arm and suddenly the red spot popped and thick green stuff like toothpaste oozed out of the opening in a continuous stream. He continued the process for about 20 minutes until about a quart of the ghastly stuff had drained from my arm. "I'll come back tomorrow and the next few days until there is no more! Meanwhile, I'm going to give you a shot of a new wonder drug called "PENICILLIN". It has just come on the market and I brought some back from the seminar I attended."

At this writing, MRSA has become one of the deadliest staff infections in the world and is immune to nearly all of the anti-biotic drugs known to man, including Penicillin and kills thousands of people every year!

Doc instructed mother to keep me in bed on my back for the next 48 hours and truss my right arm up over my head in a makeshift sling. He told her how to give me a shot and she was to give me one every 4 hours for the next 48 hours. Three days later the infection was gone and within one week I was back playing baseball, tennis and golf like nothing had happened to me. Doctor Rodgers was a miracle worker! How did he know about this new drug when the high priced specialists at Munson hospital didn't? How did he know how to use it and save my arm while the specialists just wanted to cut it off? Was all of this just a coincidence or was it something else or some higher force at work here? To this day I believe that his skill and his faith in God and mine as well empowered him to do God's work. He not only saved my arm but he saved my life as well and I will never forget him. <u>I truly believe he was one of my life's angels!</u>

As I write this book at my age in my seventies, it is glaringly obvious that Guardian Angels have looked over and protected me many times in my lifetime. On several occasions I have been on the very brink of death only to somehow miraculously escape completely unscathed! How can this be? There must be a reason in God's scheme of things and the good Doctor Rodgers certainly played a part in it!

B.L.

2/2008

EPILOGUE

The author went on to college at Michigan State University for a period of three years where I studied Commercial Art and played baseball under an athletic scholarship. In 1953 I quit school to play professional baseball until I was drafted into the army. I had lost my deferred status during the Korean War. As luck would have it, the draft turned me down due to medical reasons and I returned home to play another year of professional baseball before meeting my beautiful wife to be, Sally. We were married, moved back to Bellaire and raised three wonderful children to adulthood before divorcing in 1982.

The town of Bellaire played a major role in the lives of two generations and the enchantment of the town still beckons me to return there to my roots every summer. Although I was born and spent my first 12 years in the Detroit area and currently live in Florida, I still consider Bellaire to be my home.